POETRY NOW
WESTERN ENGLAND 2002

Edited by

Natalie Nightingale

First published in Great Britain in 2002 by
POETRY NOW
Remus House,
Coltsfoot Drive,
Peterborough, PE2 9JX
Telephone (01733) 898101
Fax (01733) 313524

Copyright Contributors 2001

HB ISBN 0 75432 740 X
SB ISBN 0 75432 741 8

FOREWORD

Although we are a nation of poets we are accused of not reading
poetry, or buying poetry books. After many years of listening to

CONTENTS

UNDISCLOSED UTOPIA

Way above the washing lines
And leafy, lilting lanes
Beyond the chintz and cherry bowls
And sugar residential names

Twitching curious curtains
Pleasing plain-faced smiles
Observe the soaring skylarks
In a quizzical candyfloss style

Lemon-coated loveliness
Adorns the great facade
A little lower than loneliness
Though prettier than prices paid

In technicolour treetops
Lie hugely hungry cats
Debating dubious decisions
While wallowing on golden mats

There's a candid crisis occurring
Betwixt the bullbars and balloons
Racing runners returning
Knowing no news is good news

Eat more cake than I can eat
Eat more cake than most
When the crumbs that will deplete
You can come share our toast.

Kevin Smette

THE CALLING

Do you hear Me whispering?
I call to you;
I wait until you miss Me
then I call.
I know your name
and your thoughts.
I know your dreams,
your hopes.
And when you think
you're all alone
you call.
You lose someone
and need to be held
or comforted,
then you reach -
you need to know
I'm here.
I wait
until you're ready
then I call.
You regret an act
or a word
and you whisper to Me
in the dead of night
so only I will hear
and I wait
till you plead.
I'll be here
but I need you to need.
Then I'll call.

Karen Barron

PIGEONS
(For Matthew)

Five years old, with the biggest stamp you could manage,
and the 'raaagh' of a hungry lion, you sprang at them.
At worst the pigeons picked up their pink legs
and scuttled away; at best they fluttered into flight,
brittle wings fanned and luminous against the low sun,
to trouble another table. But always, like worries,
they returned, ducking and strutting just too near
to be ignored, nagging the gravel for crumbs, tenacious
as unruly thoughts, like wondering if the bears
beneath the pavement lines will come for you.

Are games genetic? I used to do this, too and once
ran free and unafraid across Trafalgar Square
through thousands of thrumming, cooing pigeons,
the passers-by chuckling, nudging and nodding.
The birds side-stepped, scuffled up and away;
and I felt I'd won, imposed myself. I remember then
I stood and threw them crumbs from a crumpled paper bag,
never asking why they grew so big or so many,
or if one day they'd turn and stare at me, hard-eyed,
insistent, unafraid of all my loudest roars.

J D Gilpin

ENTERING THE WORLD

When you enter the world it's a big surprise.
When you get older you start to realise life isn't what it's meant to be.
It's just a test everyone tries to be better than the rest.
There's the posh ones, the poor ones, the ones that don't care.
The good, bad and greedy will always be there.
But when the time comes and judging is done
We will see all these bad ones wanting to run.
Because life is just a test and nobody but nobody is better than the rest.

Donna Kelly

TUESDAY SEPTEMBER 11TH 2001 ABOUT 8.50AM

A morning warm and clear azure
With greetings 'Hi' and loving care
A gentle drone to start this day
Then the shattering nightmare
Terror came and awoke a nation
Now the search is on for information
For all America needs an answer
To a catastrophic annihilation
Two ridged fingers, a victory sign
Came crashing to the floor
A sign of hope and glory
Lay shattered and is no more!
The death knell of the reaper
Scythed through New York City
Now its people stunned with shock and horror
Must mourn its dead and show courageous pity
Do not despair of a dastardly act
For time will heal and you'll be back
The victory fingers will be bigger and better
And all America will rejoice, rejoice!

Eugene Cummings

OUR WORLD

Things around us change dramatically yet do we really care?
We dump chemicals into the sea and help pollute the air.
This will finally cause the death of us, but we are only to blame,
We must stop this destruction or life will never be the same.

A tree that helps us breathe, we cut it down in haste,
Forsaking all its living things and this is such a waste.
We will destroy this world of ours and there'll be devastation,
For we'll wipe out the human race, one of our Lord's creations.

Neale John Harrison

MRS CHRISTMAS

All alone sat quietly in the corner,
no noise, no movement,
sitting very, very still.
Then with a flick of a switch
she blinks her many twinkling eyes
and she wakes up.
A breeze gently flows into the room
and sends a shudder around her
drooping shoulders.
The coloured dots on her dress
gently sway, slowly, slowly.
Her arms stretch out
to reach her foot
trapped and held down
by large multicoloured slippers.
Slowly the slippers are taken away
her bare leg stands lonely and cold,
her dress just covers her knee
but she glows a warmth of love.
And on her head her hat
pointed and bright
glows like a flame
on this cold Christmas night.

Linda Francis

PERCEPTIONS

When I was young I dreamt I'd live 'happy ever after' . . .
That every day would be filled up
With song and dance and laughter!

When I was young I dreamt I'd be a prima ballerina
I'd dance with stardust in my toes
And kings would boast 'I've seen her' . . .

When I was young I thought I'd have a mansion and a chauffeur
But now I'm old, it's sad to say
That hasn't happened - so far!

When I was young . . . *if* I were young -
I'd stop my silly dreaming, and know that pleasure's not in wealth
In bank rolls that lay gleaming
But - in life's simple things; little treasures all around . . .
Like friends who pop along for tea
That's the kind of wealth for me
When sweet surprises lie in store
For with such wealth, no one is 'poor'!

Hannah Yates

SMALL BROWN MOUSE

Stretching lazily in the morning sun
The sleek black cat wakens to the sound of time,
Eternally progressing in slight discord.
Her back gently arches, her peaked ears twitch
Her almond shaped eyes slowly dilate
To the wondrous depth of large green orbs.
Sharp teeth gleam as she licks with rough pink tongue
Her glossy coat, until ablutions are done.
Hesitantly she steps with dainty stride
Over the stony path to the outside gate,
Tail standing tall, then swishing aside.
Seeing her prey she crouches down low
Then lifelessly still, she stares at her foe,
Eye to eye in cold mesmerising glare.
Suddenly pouncing, cruel claws extending
She tosses her prey playfully up in the air
Catching and circling, leaping and bending,
Running and dancing without seeming to care.

The stony path stains a bright crimson red.
The small brown mouse is now horribly dead.

Isobel M Maclarnon

TRIAL SEPARATION

It seemed that happiness had fled
to some dark place for refuge; and fulfilment too.
The house is blind and silent as a stone,
with daylight fading and the summer gone.

I fall through darkness many hopeless years
in this day's space:
seeking an echo, finding none.
The memory of your parting gaze seems years away.
Dream upon dream becomes illusion,
to convince me you alone are real:
and night must end at last and dawn embrace.

Michael Limmer

SILENT CHURCHES OF VENICE

St George in a boyish pose,
still now in salted depths,
drowned in this drowning city
by the warming of the world.

Silent churches in calm waters
immortality on walls of painted silence
small fish mulching holy mysteries
billowing truth in a moist Eden.

Sinner and saint
triumph and death
resurrection and death
the son is saved
but
his world is melting
the world is sinking
returning and rejoining
the silent waters
of the deep.

John Spencer

St Helier

Jackboots, raised arms,
unsmiling faces:
unwelcome strangers
marching down
sun-washed streets

Passing the prim tea shop,
Matthews Ironmongers,
town hall clock,
the horse-chestnut tree
whose roots crack the pavement

Fifty years on
the familiarity of those buildings
startles me; and I shudder
at the faint photograph, and
what might have come thereafter.

Catherine Bradbury

HER GOLDEN GIRL

Emma's mother lifts the gold leaf carefully
with her finest brush.
She shows me how it flakes and powders
at the slightest heavy handedness
or floats away if you let your breath out.

She is learning to illuminate.

Emma goes for her monthly gold injection.
Her doctor, a beneficent Midas, works his alchemy.
Visit by visit, her stiff joints unfurl like ferns.
She lets her breath out carefully, aware that,
just as suddenly, Midas could turn malicious.

She is learning to hope.

Emma's mother lifts the gold leaf carefully.
She imagines as she concentrates that, oh so gently,
she is gilding her daughter's precious limbs with love.
Her golden girl unfolds from sleep into the Magi gift
of a bright and pain-free morning.

She is illuminated.

Carolyn Garwes

THE UNKNOWN POET

Oh what a gem I found
Within each faded page.
Beautifully decorated and golden bound,
Verses that never age.
Words forever will bring
Like chapters of a book unfold.
Precious as a diamond ring.
Now in my hands I hold
A book to read in a still night.
Favourites they recall
Sheer delight.
Like watching the first snowflakes fall
Or swans swimming on a crystal lake, a moment rare.
That's why I love to read these verses again,
Left forever to share.
Inspired through innocence then
Left a gift to treasure too
That come from the heart,
Leave me wondering anew.
Send spirits soaring like a lark
Must have felt some joy
Of reflections of childhood days
Paint the blue clear sky
And wild flowers greet with praise
A time when time stood still it seems.
Memories to treasure
Fulfilling wishes and dreams.
Full of untold pleasure
But this a poetry book I find
Where the question always remains
Who wrote such lovely lines?

Maureen Anne Hanmer

THE NURSE

The nurses greet you with a pleasant smile
As they walk up and down the hospital aisle,
Caring for your every whim and need.
Bringing you breakfast, supper, tea.

Doing the rounds to check your well-being
Providing a pot for your willy to pee in,
Medicine cabinet crawls its way round
Supplying relief when pain gets you down.

Light hearted chat to suppress the boredom
Little red button, just press to call 'em,
Bringing comfort as you recuperate in bed
Checking your pulse, making sure you're not dead.

Working all hours, both night and day
Deserving a medal and a lot more pay,
For their service is priceless, the good old nurse
But when comes the enema I don't fancy being first.

Paul Axtell

A Day In The Life Of A Waitress

The 'bus is late, and the threatening rain starts to descend,
That this lifts my leaden spirits I cannot pretend.

It's Monday morning and I am travelling to work,
The week's bad start tempts me my duties to shirk.

Only customers have problems, so I forget the journey when I arrive,
And paint on a smile, my acting ability nobody can despise.

Having affixed that curve to my lips, I start serving straight away,
I might begin to feel sorry for myself with any further delay.

Customers do behave badly, both children and adults,
But we who serve, are not allowed to find faults.

A small boy shouts and aims a kick at me,
Because his mother refuses him a knickerbocker glory.

Too much, too little, too hot, too cold, wrong colour, they complain,
But I am accustomed to holding my temper on a tight rein.

I spill hot soup and nobody knows if unintentional or meant,
But I can assure that loud-mouthed yuppie it was no accident.

Every language spoken I am expected to understand,
Occasionally tourists' insolence begs the back of my hand.

Other times honest mistakes with English make me laugh,
Hot bread for toast, open wood for door, head cover for scarf.

With all the ups and downs behind, this day ends like so many before,
Travelling home I feel as if I've fought a mini war.

I climb off the 'bus, and decide tomorrow, I will resign,
But can I be sure that for my job as a waitress I will not pine?

Relaxing with feet up I realise I was not thinking straight,
I would miss not knowing what you choose to be on your plate.

So I am settling for the lot I've got no duress,
Dine at our restaurant and be served by this happy waitress.

Joy R Gunstone

TWINKLE TOES

My feet are in disagreement,
Don't know my left from my right.
Can't tell a waltz from a tango,
When I take the floor, what a sight.

I thought I would have dancing lessons,
To improve my image with birds,
When I do a fox-trot or samba,
My partners are quite lost for words.

My teacher said, 'We have a problem,
Your feet have a mind of their own,
Perhaps if they spoke to each other,
You wouldn't be dancing alone.'

I bought special shoes, quite expensive,
They fit like a glove, second skin,
But when I tried dancing a cha-cha,
I just kicked myself on the shin.

Then I decided a quickstep
Would wow all the girls with my grace,
The quickstep turned into a trip step
As I fell flat on my face.

Determined that I would conquer,
My dyslexic feet, so to speak,
Took off my shoes and changed over,
Put them on the opposite feet.

They now call me John Travolta,
My teacher says, 'This is a first,
You dance every dance to perfection,
Whilst doing them all, in reverse.'

Jim Sargant

AUTUMNS PAST

Autumn's colours, gathered conkers
Soaked in vinegar, baked till hard
Frosty mornings, accessories needed
Coats, hats, gloves and scarves.

Laces tied and hankies in pockets
Dear little boys all in a row
Hugs and kisses were lovingly given
Pile out the door, away we go.

Along the road we quickly walk
Turn around to just make sure
They're still with me in graduation
Yes, they're there 1,2,3,4.

Spirits high and laughter's flowing
Anticipation of the coming day
I look on and ponder slowly
As each departs to his own way.

Just a morning of daily life
A few years back, I thought would last
The happy years we spent together
Before they grew to boys of past.

Last dear little boy of a hand to hold
I treasure every second until it's time
To step back and watch, just like his brothers
When a man he becomes, I'll fall behind.

Joy Susan Cotton

UNTITLED

On summer nights across the vale
Such goings-on do prevail
Of Morris men country dancing
Old men, young girls, all a prancing
Such scenes as this bring so much joy
To the hearts of every girl and boy.

People gather from all around,
Such merrymaking does abound
Beers bought in from the Cotswold way
Many will be tasted this festival day.
Old Spot, Sarah; names such as these
Bring old and young alike to their knees.

Old men sit and reminisce
When they were young on days like this
So much has changed, you hear them say,
When we were young on festival day.

A E Wallington

THE VISITORS

Dawn came on feathered wings and sang at my window . . .
Her song so charmed the sun that he rose, golden, glorious;
Warm was his touch upon my face . . .
And he came not alone
For with him came *day*

Dusk came as deepening velvet with violet hues;
His cool sweetness clothed me, soft and quiet,
Calm was his touch upon my soul . . .
And he was not alone
For with him came *night*

You came, with clear blue eyes and sun-kissed face,
Grey and golden your hair, your arms so strong . . .
We were together, folding, melting,
Very souls entwined in dear delight . . .
And you came not alone
My sweet, my darling,
For with you came *love*.

Una Davies

WHY?

The softly spoken voice pierces my swollen heart
Like a bolt of lightning
Each sentence, each word, each syllable, each letter,
Tears through my warm, soft flesh

All my hopes and dreams ooze slowly to the cold, hard floor
All my love and devotion trickles painfully over my still fleshy mound

Thundering silence envelopes me as scalding tears burn my ashen face
My paralysed voice screams out in pain,
My sunken body lies hysterically still

No movement, no motion,
Just insane madness pulsating through my every vein

No sound, no clamour,
Just a violent halo of shrill reticence vibrating inside my head

Condemnation creeps through my thoughts,
Cursing me, cursing you, cursing me again
Cursing the deadliness that surrounds me

I feel obsession for more and more excruciating pain
I want to see my emotional and physical pain;
I want to punish my angry, raging existence

These feelings crush me
Frustration surrounds me

No response to my questions
When? How? Why?

Oh how I plead in desperation for the answers
Why, oh why, oh why?

When did this tiny life inside me . . .

How did this tiny life inside me . . .

Why did this tiny life inside me . . .

. . . suddenly lie so still?

Catarina Godwin

IN THE SHADOW OF A BEAUTY

In the shadow
Of a beauty I stand.
Can you see me
As I hold out my hand?
Do I sparkle in the
Corner of your eye?
Like a star
In a beautiful sky.

In the shadow
Of a beauty I smile.
Do I hold your attention?
Do you stay for a while?
Do you see past the day
And look into the night?
She is the lighthouse
Am I the light?

In the shadow
Of a beauty I walk.
I feel you listening
As I start to talk.
You pull me from the darkness
And as I stand on my own.
You take the crown from the queen
And give me the throne.

Liz Perrin

FREDERICK MOTH

Frederick Moth stood on the ceiling today
Warming himself by the bulb.
Preening his wings, he would turn and would sway,
Thinking of flies he could hold.

On looking down he noticed the bath,
Full of warm water and 'her'.
'Hee, hee,' he said softly and started to laugh,
And got ready to frighten the girl.

He took one last kick from the ceiling of flies,
Judging his distance and aim,
He flew past her arms, her toes and her thighs,
Just missing her, again and again.

The more she cried 'No,' the more he would go.
Brushing her legs, mouth and ears.
Flapping his wings, dive bombing her toe
'Til she was so near to tears.

On one of these trips came a sad demise,
The girl, she started to laugh.
For Frederick collided with one of the flies,
And poor thing, he was drowned in the bath!

Jolie Marchant

MOTORWAY SERVICES

Some have had troubled journeys.
Their faces, staring into reflecting windows,
dread the miles still to go.

Others travel light, shrug off the dark,
lean and sway with the road -
Like the bikers,

leathered, weathered,
conscious of their distance from
the family man,

who would have driven much harder
and got there sooner if it weren't for
the wife and kids:

They eat in silence; the baby, sleeping,
has yet to learn how tired she can be.
That group, all in black, are

travelling to a funeral; their silences are caught
with laughter; short, frequent, louder than
the rugby team.

The lethargic, uniformed staff
move from table to table,
picking up pieces of other people's lives.

Stranded; until the hour strikes
and they go home.
Home is a memory here.

Off-cuts in lives not being anywhere
but knowing where they want to be and
how long it will take if there are no hold ups.

The journey will be made:
Some are hours from its end.
Others will travel years, decades

before they're home.

Kate Leatherdale

LA PETITE ENFANT

She looked so tall
So slim
And so, so beautiful.
But nobody could see
Inside
Her head.
Because, she never said.
She felt so bad
So sad
And so dreadfully alone.
But nobody would know,
Because
She never said.
They said she acted up
Played around
And did some stuff.
But nobody would know
Because she never said.
Then they painted her up
Pushed her onto the stage
An innocent child
Trapped
In Aladdin's cave.
But then they found her
Drunk
And overdosed.
They left her
For dead.

Andrea Adsett

MEMORIES OF CHILDHOOD

Lupins in the garden, tall and stately,
Smelling of spice and pepper.
Cowslips in the hedgerows, pale yellow.
Always the same smell, year after year.
Hot summer days with the sun beating down.
Wearing brown leather sandals, T-shirt and shorts,
But still too hot.
Cool welcoming woods with their shady trees,
Do I remember any rainy days
In these summers long gone?
There were some I'm sure when we couldn't go out.
We sailed the sea in a table turned upside down.
Played hide and seek in so many hidey-holes.
Did I really fit into that tiny cupboard?
Then the rain stopped. We were out again.
Freedom we had to run and play,
To fish for newts, minnows, tadpoles.
Freedom to climb the highest trees,
To paddle in the cooling stream.
Where has our freedom gone?
Gone with out lost childhood?
Or is it still there to take hold of if we will?
Sometimes I snatch at this illusive freedom
And hold on to it for a while.
Then all childhood's memories come flooding back.
For a while I return to the carefree days of innocence.
Then back to the harsh adult world of worry and care.
Yet now I know I can return when I wish,
To the land of childhood,
When I am alone in a quiet place.

Cathy Franklin

A YEAR HAS PASSED

(Dedicated to my husband on our first anniversary 23/8/98)

A year has passed,
To the day,
That you and I had our say.

We told one and all,
That you and I,
Would be together 'til our dying day.

With everyone in the church,
Poised to hear,
The words we spoke,
With maybe just a little fear,
I think our words came loud and clear.

With the ceremony over,
Our new life began,
And my, oh my, did it start with a bang!

With the celebrations underway,
It was time for Dad to have his say,
He pulled it off,
As I knew he would,
With as much whisky as he possibly could!

At the top table,
Sat side by side,
It was the beginning of a turning tide,
I felt so happy,
I cannot explain,
The emotions ran through me,
Like torrential rain.

So here we are,
A year to the day,
And without a doubt,
I can honestly say,
With you, forever, I want to stay.

Zoe Lancelott

ST PETER'S BENTHAM

St Peter's Bentham stands so lonely, so sad to see
nestles quietly with the trees at the foot of Crickley hill,
no more those country folk inside on bended knee
wouldst your walls echo to the sound of organ still.

Standing there so proud with lofty spire
empty now, no bells to call - no sound of feet,
missing within you the soft voices of a choir
still someone cares - to come and keep graveyard neat.

You still stand dutiful as the Lord's sentinel
left in contemplation without voice or sound,
as if you are that great holy citadel
guardian to those who sleep beneath the ground.

Like St Peter guardian of heaven's golden gate
who stands smiling to welcome the blessed flock,
you St Peter stand martyr to your fate
just quietly watching, timeless as your clock.

Jon Arden

SHOES FOR THOUGHT

High heels, low heels
Cuban heels - flats
square toes, pointed toes
some with sling backs
light blue, powder blue,
royal blue - navy
some with spots, pierced through dots
or pretty lines - wavy.
Loafers, moccasins, platforms - daps!
Plain ones, posh ones,
fancy ones with straps
old styles, new styles - I've each -
without a doubt!
Hey! No! I can't stop now -
They're always bringing new styles out!

Delia Mason

WONDERFUL PLACE

Live your life without sin
You will laugh, you will smile
You will grin.
Enraged with hate
And overpowered by greed
Live your life of wrongdoing
And you will not succeed.
If you are indulged with misery
Don't expect self pity.
It can be crowded in the country
And lonely in the city.

For it's nice to be important
But more important to be nice
You don't have to be too religious
You don't have to have too much faith.
Just remember Mother Earth,
Is your birth and dying place.
So show your respect
And don't destroy this wonderful place.

M A Medley

DONATE

Come and give blood, I'm sure you can,
You don't have to be 'Desperate Dan'.
If you are hale and fit,
Come and do your little bit.

Save the life of someone you don't know,
A little prick is all you will show,
In a couple of days it will go
And in your heart you will glow.

Rest a while before you leave,
A biscuit and a cup of tea,
Maybe you prefer coffee,
Return in four months and welcome be.

Brian Wall

THE ROSE THAT DEATH GAVE

The fetid son of madness
Was chewing on my brain.
The vile thoughts like fireballs from hell,
Fell upon my feelings like the rain.

His eyes, they pierce my cranium
And twisted my nerves until I was insane.
Soon, I had become a gibbering mess . . .
Empty of thought, and so vain!

Masquerading thoughts of doom
So exquisitely entertain!
While Satan collected some passengers
From off the sinner train.

The 'thought' was non-existence.
The 'fact' was intense pain.
And a newly born life
Will very shortly wane.

Like flowers without water,
Or a virgin on Satan's altar.
Like the corpses lying in the ground,
Or the snarls of a demonic hound!

The bolt of lightning that struck your heart
And the evil one who tore your soul apart.
Into a fetish, they thrust pins
And inflected pain into your evil eye
So that sin
Would truly die!

Wake to another day.
Madness has done its job,
And requested no pay!
Satan has your soul
And he leads it away
To an unending night
Which used to be another day.
It is in there
That you will stay . . .
Forever!

The rose that death gave
Was the fantasy you crave,
And the shovel that dug your grave!

Peter Steele

MUM'S WASHING LINE

The wind is darting in a sprightly dance,
to dry the washing, the perfect chance.
Summer's azure blue, puffy clouds on high,
not a hint of rain spoils a beautiful sky.

See Dad's green shirt, how its sleeves entwine
with Mum's best blouse with the buttons that shine.
How they twist and shake to a very fast number,
or could it be that they do the rumba?

Watch Tim's woolly socks which he wears with his boots,
for walking his dogs on their country pursuits,
give a cheery wave, as he gives Kizzy a whistle,
to call her to heel, trekking hill, grass and thistle.

Then the wind with a flutter and a soft caress,
gently blows out the creases in Becky's nurse's dress,
for it seems to feel that we all should share,
in the work of those who for the sick all care.

Now the wind with a rush and a hearty puff
and an admiring tug to Shaun's designer 'stuff',
dries his Burberry top and his Ralph Lauren,
which he keeps for best, donning now and then!

Sometimes, Mum feeling sad, sheds a few little tears,
recalling with love all the long gone years,
the lines of clean nappies so fluffy and white,
for three little people who woke her at night.

Longing to feel them in her arms again,
with their soft, sweet freshness, until smiling then
she thinks to herself, 'They've all turned out fine,
with the help of the wind and my washing line!'

Sylvia Gwilliam

ONE FOR SORROW

It lies within the hollow, crouching low,
Like some grave-wounded beast of prey.
Its darkened eyes, all grime-encrusted now
Stare blindly out. On its mad way
The world, unheeding, rushes by.

The sun is sinking fast, its golden ray
Lights up those eyes like lamplight's glow.
I think I hear within a fiddle play
The haunting tunes of long ago,
Those songs still loved as time goes by.

Laughter grows louder now as drink flows free,
And drowned in raucous merriment
The fiddle's note. Then sudden tragedy;
A knife blade glints. Its swift descent
Cuts down a life. Death claims his prey.

The borrowed glow is fading from blind eyes,
The kind full moon with softer light
Will soon send down from clear, star-spangled skies
Its beams to bathe the forlorn site
With silver. The night breezes sigh.

Pale shades sigh too, dark timbers creak and groan,
'The Lion Couchant' restless lies.
From moss-clad roof a screech-owl's eerie tone
Disturbs the dusk. Through velvet skies
I see a lonely magpie fly.

K B Law

COTSWOLD VIEWS

For fifty years I've enjoyed the view out there 'neath the eastern sky.
The rural scene changes with the seasons, e'er pleasing to the eye.
Where the ground dips to Stroudwater valley, passing traffic reflects
the sun's rays.
Straight ahead on a clear day, across the vale, a hillside church meets
my gaze.

But enhancing the scene are the Cotswolds; those high blue hills
poets recall.
They climb and they dip, then twist and turn as round Stroud's
five valleys they sprawl.
And as I watch the new day dawning, a pink glow shines through
clouds of grey,
As behind those hills the rising sun greets the morn with a rosy display.

Once more as night is falling my eye to the Cotswolds strays,
I see the rings of orange lamps adjacent to our highways.
On a distant slope there's a splash of brightness as hospital
windows gleam,
While around and about the twinkling hillside lights complete
the scene.

Jocelyn Lander

Up Above And Down Below

The stars and planets in the sky
Up in orbit, flying high,
Some are big, some are small,
But all the same shape, a big, bright ball.

No one knows how they got there,
Or indeed if they will stay.
Fingers crossed, hope and pray
And wish upon the Milky Way.

Indeed, ourselves we live upon a stone
And our bodies are formed upon bone.
Where did we come from and where will we go?
This is something none of us know.

And on life's journey we will all stumble,
But this is good as it makes you humble,
Take time to recollect,
Start again and earn respect.

Look back at where you went wrong.
Look inside yourself. This will make you strong.
Strong enough to face life's peril,
The strength to shun the Devil.

You'll do wrong, you'll do good,
But as long as you understood,
Be patient and do not curse,
As we all live in this universe.

Karl Dewick

A DAY AT WESTON-SUPER-MARE

Weston days are here again,
I am going down by train,
Lots of sun and lots of space,
I am having chips and plaice.
Everything's so nice and cheap,
In my purse, I'll not dig deep.
The Weston people are so nice,
I think I'll stop and have an ice.
The tide is out, but never fear,
I'll take a walk along the pier,
I'll pat the donkeys on the sand,
They'll nuzzle me and lick my hand.
I'll have a ride on the little land train,
The sun is out, it will not rain,
The tide's coming in, there's sand in my hair,
I'll not worry, I haven't a care.
It's time to leave, my train is here,
Goodbye Weston – till next year.

Elizabeth Woodham

PEELING POTATOES

I feel good when I peel a spud.
I'm doing someone a favour,
So they can enjoy and savour
A well-peeled potato flavour.
For me it is a painful sight
When they're gobbled in one big bite.
Eat them with love and gentleness
And enjoy their sweet tenderness.
Some people say, 'Eat the skin,
Lots more goodness is therein.
To peel potatoes is a sin.'
But you don't know where
That spud has been.
I stand and peel spuds all day long,
With that there can't be nothin' wrong.
Machine-peeled spuds make me shudder,
Cos I'm a peeled-potato lover.
I could quickly lose my job,
Spud-peeling machines could rob
And take away my living.
When peeled in haste, they lose their taste
And my a-peeling love I'll stop giving.
To show my professional skill
And explain peeling spuds at will,
Unless you're a potato hater,
All I need is a commen-tator.

Norman Holmes

THE WANDERER'S RETURN

There is no village thick with houses
No organised conflicting scheme
There never was and never will be
Ways will always be the same

This is a landscape as no other
No fantasies to mar the scene
One can predict that all in future
Will remain as it has been

Wherein a native long uprooted
Drifts dreamily upon return
Through avenues long since forsaken
Was it to err these ways to spurn?

Here thrives the very thing unblemished
The harmony that breeds content
Splendour lies within its pattern
Yet to better it is why he went.

Jack Pritchard

VIEW FROM MY BED (ANGLESEY)

I awaken, as she throws back the drapes.
The mists intermingle the stems of sunlight,
Dappled streak across ashen, hoary boulders.
Scrubland shrubs and vegetation house little creatures,
Keeping their own counsel apart from us.
Coarse grassland gives up its flora and fauna,
Displaying their hues and bee-laden trumpets.
Horses trot to and fro across the headland,
Skirting beyond wind-swept trees.
A heron rises from sap-filled reeds.
One of us spies a quick slither of a weasel.
Rabbits sit poised at a wanted scent or is it foe?
A hare, seldom seen, meets the range of our field glasses.
We view with great pleasure at his strength and size.
He darted, sat and lorded over his domain.
Birds dived and soared,
Larks on the 'up and up' to uppermost skies,
Swallows ready for the 'off',
Magpies furtively eating nature's debris.
Bullocks flicking flies, chew nonchalantly.
Sleepy ewes lie under stone walls and blackberry hedges.
Insects hover in the air.
I absorb all this tranquillity.
Suddenly,
Two jets shatter the space,
And my peace, with ear-splitting screams.

Lin Legerton

IT'S HAPPENED

It's happened, hoped it wouldn't,
You have left my life forever,
With you, you took my heart.

Seven years have passed,
We've had good times and bad,
But something pulled us through,
My love for you is still true,
I had to let you go,
You don't love me like you used to.

I couldn't watch you walk away.
Though I tried not to cry,
I couldn't stop the tears,
Now I'm full of fears,
How can I go on without you?

It's happened, you've gone to her,
She has all of you now.
I hope she loves you like I do
And takes care of you too,
Supports you when you're blue.
Never forget I love you.

Sheridan Perrie

MAY MORNING

Woken at dawn by the first trill of birdsong,
Soon the full choir is assembled to sing,
Welcoming in this lovely May morning,
Each note announcing the crowning of spring.

Mist on the meadows, a silvery blanket
Covers the grass, with flowers bursting through,
Golden and starry-white, sparkling with dewdrops,
Raising their faces to skies turning blue.

Down through the long lace-edged paths we can wander,
May-blossom trailing its beauty from trees;
Rich white cascades, like bridal wreaths swaying,
Vibrant green branches all dance in the breeze.

Down in the shadows, the bluebells are blooming,
Blue sea of beauty, a rest for the soul,
Shaded by ferns with their green fronds uncurling –
Nature's spring carpet, a harmonious whole.

And as we walk, we can share this abundance
With passing strangers, enhancing its charm;
Sharing the sights, sounds and scents of the season,
Sharing the pastoral peace and the calm.

Wondering, I ask, was it on a May morning,
So long ago, on a faraway hill,
When Love was given, so precious and costly,
Love for His sheep and lambs, guarding us still?

Joy Jenkins

FELIX THE FISHERMAN

Felix the fisherman lives close to the sea
oft he would go to catch fish for his tea
big and burly and stout is he
long he would wait to catch his tea

and when his moment of triumph arrived
he hauled his line but the fish dived
back into the sea he swam again
and Felix filled with rage threw again

his fishing line back into the sea
he waited and waited patiently
he felt a tug and hoisted his line
shouted at last my tea this time

he reeled his line back to the shore
took out the hook from the fish's jaw
and gazing at the fish once more

the fish glared back with his glassy eyes
and oh how he seemed to hypnotize
strangely he threw the fish back into the sea
gathered his things and left no fish for tea.

Patricia A Taylor

UNTITLED

Don't cry at my grave or stand and stare
Because my soul will not be there.
I'll be in heaven with those I love,
We'll all be watching you from above.
Please remember I love you all,
I knew one day that God would call,
I've loved my family all my life,
But most of all I love my wife.
We've had our rows in our wedded bliss,
But we always forgave with a loving kiss.

Please don't mourn or shed a tear,
Although I've gone I will still be near.
Please don't rush for I can wait
And I'll meet you at St Peter's gate,
We'll hug and kiss while I show you around,
For happiness again we'll both have found.

We'll both unite with my darling mother,
For I see her there with my dearest brother,
In a garden of love we'll all be there
With our loving family everywhere,
So don't forget, don't mourn or cry,
For I'll be with you, standing by.

If you go first when it's time to part,
I soon will follow with a broken heart.
I love you so much it causes pain,
For one day darling, we will meet again.

R R Gilbert

SEWING

Zoom! Zoom! Goes my sewing machine
I'm getting fed up with yellow and green
But never mind it's nearly done
Then I can go out and have some fun.

Beryl Tomkinson

A MOMENT IN MY TIME

Some people come and some people go,
The tide of life does ebb and flow.
Yes, people drift into this life of mine,
Leaving footprints in the sands of my time.
Some people are rare and hard to find,
But they make an impression on my mind.
They flash inspiration and I wait for the roll
As their thunder rumbles inside my soul.
These episodes of much significance,
Are they planned, or accidental in circumstance?
That fleeting glimpse, that glancing blow,
As some people come and some people go.

Gillian Khandelwal

POETRY

I'm not someone of many words.
Sometimes I find I can't be heard.
My voice is just a whisper carried in the breeze.
My face a sad expression that nobody can see.

Yet when I write a poem.
I'm an author, I'm a star.
And I can reach so many people.
No matter where they are.

The words they flow like water.
In a constant, flowing stream.
And when I write them down.
People know just what I mean.

No longer am I looked upon.
With a vacant, empty look.
When the words are flowing.
I feel I could sit and write a book.

So I'll carry on my writing.
As every day goes by.
And watch as people read my words.
Should they laugh or should they cry.

Lynn Brown

FAIR LADY

She sits on the wall, afraid and alone,
No more discomfort, just sadness she owns.
She misses the heart that she once gave away,
He gave it back broken and left her that day.

She cries in the moonlight for someone to care,
The dreams that she whispers remain in the air,
The wind it will carry them far, far away,
For he gave it back broken and left her that day.

So sad is this picture, her face pointed down,
Her fragments of laughter now formed to a frown
And her wishes and daydreams have turned to despair,
For he gave it back broken, and he did not care.

Lindsay McIlree

SLEEP

Darkness, oh ye cloak of night
Invade my senses, dim all light,
Lead my tiring eye and sleepy brain
To once each night all emotions drain.
The mind-dulled body 'neath cover lies,
Above, a blanket of star-filled skies,
And moonbeams glow a pillow make,
'Neath a mantle of silence, sleep to take,
Till the sun-stained clouds caress my face,
While impending dawn the shadows chase,
And the whispering breeze stirs the air
To awaken me to this world so fair.

G Wright

SMILING

Smiling is infectious,
You catch it like the 'flu.
When someone smiled at me today,
I started smiling too.

I passed around a corner
And someone saw me grin,
And when I smiled, I realised
I'd passed it on to him.

I thought about this smile a lot
And realised its worth.
A single smile like mine and yours
Could travel round the earth.

So if you feel a smile begin,
Don't leave it undetected,
Let's all start an epidemic
And get the world infected.

C A Storer

MY HOLIDAY IN MENORCA

It is August the 11th, six in the morning,
We are tired and drowsy and also yawning.

We've got a flight to Menorca, we can't wait,
So we'd better hurry, we can't be late.

We got to the airport, got on the plane,
We had to wait over an hour to go, what a shame.

We got there safely, straight in the pool
Because it was so hot, I needed to cool.

We go to the club to talk to some friends
Because we haven't got long till the holiday ends.

So off we go to have some fun,
Lying down in the sun.

The two weeks are over, it's goodbye to Spain,
Back home to England and the pouring rain.

Tanya Cherrington (11)

FAMILY LIFE

Life is a gamble, of that we all know,
The kids are all screaming – when can we go?
All washing is done, the cleaning is too,
Oh, do I have time to go to the loo?

Time is precious or so they say,
We must make most time to be happy and gay.
A laugh, a joke is always a tonic,
Why are there people who can be so chronic?

We know and accept that good health is a must,
So why can't we live in harmony and trust?
As for wealth, it can cause more harm than good,
I fancy a gamble – do you think I should?

Winning or losing they say it's all fair,
I'm always reflecting whilst doing my hair.
The days are too short, the nights can be long,
Let's raise our glasses, let's have a song.

Down with the miseries, up with the glad,
Let's all be happy instead of being sad.
We all need love and we all need care,
Our parents and families are something to share.

In living of live, we must take risks,
But let's not go mad and do things for kicks.
We all have the gift to care and to love,
So let's all give thanks to our Maker above.

R J Hetherington

To My Special Son

God has sent you to me, a gift from up above
He said that you were so unique and needed very special love,
And even through some days I find the job a bit too hard to bear,
I know life would be unbearable for me, if you weren't there.

No one except God really knows why things are so hard for you,
Or why you can't do all the things that other children do.
Who cares if you can't read or write or say things always understood,
The fact is, when you want to, all you do or say is really good.

One day, though, when I'm older and can't be there for you,
I pray someone else will take my place and love you like I do.
I hope that in these coming years, I can prepare you for this time,
But never, ever forget, my love, you always will be mine.

I know that I should thank God who gave my son to me,
He must have given it a lot of thought and put his trust in me,
So now, however tough it gets, you know how much I care,
For no one will ever take your place . . .
You're my son, I love you and always will be there.

Wendy Harrison

GRACE

We sit, we think and wonder why,
We contemplate life and give a sigh,
The hurts we've known are on our mind,
Perhaps life could have been a little more kind.

Of the nasty moments, we surely keep score
And wish of the good times you could have known more.
But stop a while and think what you've got –
A beautiful girl with a big, curly mop.

There's no price on earth that could ever replace
The love that shines from her little face.
She keeps for her mommy her cheekiest smiles,
More precious than a jar full of pearls.

Her radiant health,
More precious than wealth,
There's no one and nothing could take the place
Of the little rascal by the name of Grace.

We never know what fate has in store,
The next step in life is an open door,
So enjoy what you've got and just let it happen,
From the day we are born, our life follows its pattern.

Freda Lyndon

EARTHQUAKE EXTRAVAGANZA

An enormous earthquake has just horrifically hit our city
I stand alone. Scared and bewildered.
Petrified people scream out for their families,
Masses of people, injured or dead
Bodies sacrificed for the ones they love,
The earthquake has caused devastating destruction,
Buildings and cars destroyed in seconds.
I can see my home crushed to pieces like the bodies around me,
Tears run down my cheek like a water fountain.
My heart breaks down like the buildings of my city.
Searching afar, I see my parents in the distance.
Terrified, I run, eager to see my parents.
With every step I take, I become weaker and weaker,
I reach out for them with my every ounce of strength I have left.
I hug them both, knowing we're all still alive.

David Smith (14)

I WILL ALWAYS BE NEAR

You may not see me, but I will always be near
To walk beside you, so you need not fear.
I am the sun in the sky, I am the rustling of leaves,
I am the footsteps you walk, I am the fluttering breeze.
I will feel your laughter, I will feel your pain,
I will carry your burdens, if it lessens your strain.
If your thoughts turn to doubt, I will brush them aside,
I will enter your head and fill you with pride.

In your quieter moments, if you're feeling alone,
Remember the seeds in your heart that I've sown.
These seeds of love, no one can take away,
They grow ever stronger with each passing day.
I am the slightest of sounds, I am the stars in the night,
I will be forever with you, even though I'm out of sight.
When the Lord calls you to him, when you're old and grey,
I will be right there beside you, to show you the way.

Sue Richards

HALLOWE'EN

'Tis witches' night, 'tis witches' night,
It's Hallowe'en, the night sky's bright.
A myriad strident voices clearly ring
As excited kids leap, dance and sing.
Their thoughts are on black, monstrous hats,
Beneath which are witches holding red-eyed cats,
On big, brushy, rough, stout-handled brooms,
Wondering will the witches fly up to the moon?
Ideas abound of the witches' wicked spells being cast,
Of being turned into a frog or toad, and how long the spell will last!
Then there's creepy, crawling hairy spiders galore,
Where are they coming from? The kids haven't espied them before.
Wheeling, dipping and diving, perhaps touching a face,
Scary, whirring, swirling, flying bats race.
Lighted, glowing pumpkin lanterns are there
Shedding eerie shadows on all. Beware!
Maybe the kids will play a game called 'Trick or Treat'?
Ring the neighbours' doorbell, run, hide away up the street.
'Tis witches' night, 'tis witches' night,
It's Hallowe'en, the night sky is bright.

Vivian Khan

SPIRIT

When I leave my body in sleep
I can float for miles
Innocent children are asleep
Nodding parents, knowing smiles
Passing over silent towns
Only secret lovers stir
Seeing night's creatures around
Sudden noises, who goes there?
Silently I pass by
Voyager in a cosmic sea
Silently above I fly
All things I can see
Drifting over freezing deserts
Passing ice fields that burn
Feeling thoughts past and present
Knowledge absorbed then to learn
Reasons why, reasons for
Answers in the void
Nights to drift and many more
Spirit journeys enjoyed.

Anthony Warwick

HANDS

God gave us hands to do His work
In many different ways.
Creative hands,
Hardworking hands;
Hands folded close to pray.
Hands outstretched in greeting,
A handshake firm and kind.
Hands that 'speak' and 'read' by touch
To help the deaf and blind.
Gentle hands that soothe and heal,
Will lift us when we fall.
Hands that bring us music,
The sweetest sound of all.
Hands that give a blessing,
With gifts from heaven above.
God gave us hands to do His work
And fill the world with love.

Cynthia Shum

GLAD IT'S ALL OVER!

It's a quarter to ten on a Saturday night,
The wife's getting pains, but she says she's all right.
She keeps tossing and turning the whole night through,
I enquire, 'How are you?' but what else can I do.
'Shall I ring the hospital?' 'No, I don't want to go.
Just wait until the morning and then I should know.'

Sunday, dawn breaks and she is still in pain,
And on top of all that, it's started to rain.
I waited till teatime and could wait no more,
'Can I use the phone?' I enquired next door.
Half-past five and we are off on our way,
Perhaps she will have it before the end of the day.
They give her a needle and she is starting to roam,
Shouting, 'How much longer?' and 'Take me back home!'

Twenty-past five on Monday morning,
She gave out a cry, without any warning.
Finger on the buzzer and a tear in her eye,
'I have wet the bed,' I heard her cry.
Down to the delivery room they carted her off,
So I retire to the drinks machine, for a cup of hot broth.

It's a quarter to six and the baby is born,
It's been thirty-two hours, I sighed with a yawn.
One hour later I am allowed in to see
What the result of those nine months turned out to be.
I'm glad it's all over, my wife cried with relief,
No more grasping of bedclothes or gritting of teeth,
The baby is all right and the wife is doing fine,
How proud I am that both of them are mine.

Don Sadler

THE AUTUMN OF OUR YEARS

The autumn's balmy days have passed
And winter's returned at last,
No doubt with cold and snow and icy blast.
Thus in the shortened days so drear,
We pray to God to expel the fear,
To be without good food and warmth
We hold so dear.
Dreaming of our youthful past,
We pray to God it's not our last.

K W Haywood

LE MANS

It's early summer and that time of year
When all our men gather all their gear.
They'll be off in their 'trannies', with plenty to drink,
The vans will be loaded, even taking a sink!
In convoy, they'll drive to catch the ferry,
By the time they get boarded, most will be merry!
A few hours more and they'll be at the track
The fun is just starting, they all know the crack!
They set up camp and collapse in a heap,
Have a look around, eat, drink, then a sleep!
A trip to the pits or a spell at the fair,
Then watch the racing, they haven't a care!
This is the pattern for the next week or so,
Until back home it's time to go.

'They're off! They've gone! Yahoo!' we cheer,
No moans, no groans, no messes to clear.
We 'racing widows' don't seem to mind
The fact that we've been left behind!
The phone starts to ring the moment they're gone
And it's down to the pub to meet everyone.
The first few days we revel with glee,
We're having such fun, it's great to be free.
We make the most of time going out
And coming home drunk with no one to shout!
The days go by, they pass much slower,
We start to miss our men with each hour.
The last day arrives and with anticipation,
We await their return, in agitation,
Enjoying the last few hours of freedom,
But we'll be ready and waiting to see them!

Patricia D Jones

DOGGIE SITTING

'We're going away for a bit,' said my son to us one day,
'We wondered, could you doggie sit while we're on holiday?'
'Of course we can,' we willingly said,
not thinking at the time we were off our head.

So dutifully we packed our bags
with nighties, crosswords, books and fags.
Each day and night our loads we'd carry
just to take care of Poppy and Harry.

I got jumped on and scratched every day,
while Cynth stayed in the lounge and kept out of the way,
no getting round Harry on that we agreed,
if he got hold of Cynth, he'd have a good feed.

Poppy, on the other hand, was really quite sweet,
she even lay by Cynthie's feet.
She came to bed with us each night,
in case we heard noises and got a fright.

Quite a few hours we wiled away,
talking of things we'd done in the day.
We painted our nails and did our hair,
a whole box of chocolates we did share.

We watched the telly and videos too,
too tired to find anything else to do.
Getting up early and going to bed late
had really taken it out of me and my mate.

All this running up and down,
no wonder I've lost over a stone,
but it's all over now, they're back today,
we hope they've enjoyed their holiday.

After two whole weeks of doing the deed,
I think a holiday is what *we* need,
so next time make it one week please,
cos we are shattered and on our knees.

Jean Cherrington & Cynthia Pitch

GOLDEN MEMORIES

Memories of long ago,
When we all had the world to go –
Friends and families, simple pleasures,
Dreams to hold
And love to treasure.
The working and the hoping,
The lives we lived, the coping,
The laughter, tears and strife,
All the daring,
And the caring –
Threads that wove us into
This 'rich tapestry' called life.

Peggy Hemmings

WINDOWS OF OUR MINDS

Falling as searing red volcanic lava,
weeping up a tidal wave.
Grief and sorrow being their spring.

Falling softly like the morning dew
shining as many faceted diamonds.
Happiness and joy they bring.

Some . . . melting hearts.
Others hardening with brittle thoughts
yet . . . without them our wells can dry up.

But these poignant tears speak
more eloquently than words ever can . . .
silently flowing from heavy hearts and fragile souls.

Margaret Kaye

THE RIDER

Amidst hazy, fog-like mist,
from the dawning grey there came to exist
a beautiful, white stallion, vibrant, full of power within its grace,
form and stride, that canters free
with sophisticated elegance before the show, with bustling,
bristling pride and dignity.

I am the Rider that humbly takes the bow,
before the applauding crowd,
that spurs the magnificent beast to do the rounds,
this noble steed, swiftly gathers speed,
turning the churning turf in tremendous leaps and bounds.

We took the first fence and the next, without fatal flaw,
to come about with mighty, pounding, heaving thrust, a perfect four.
Took what came next to leave our opponents vexed
as the clocked ticked by, good the time
and stood they in awe o'er our grandeur, aloof, beyond and sublime.
Arise The Spirit of Freedom, the exalted kind,
for soon, my galloping beauty, victory was bound to come.
Be thine and mine.

And now at last, whip stick to horses hide,
agility, power, swiftly thunders the horses hooves,
with zest the stallion quickly moves,
his body crouches as we approach, last-ditch jump adjoined by a
                                                    rumbling stream,
reaching high for the sky, kingly eminence of highest esteem:
cut the air like racing scud,
when I know for sure my horse ain't there?
To rocket earthward bound with tremulous thud
and like a splitting, cracking conker, I bang my bonger and wish
my head was made of wood! So ends the dream!

Glenwyn Evans

ADVERTS ON THE TELLY

The adverts on the telly
And nudes upon page three
Are producing in the nation
Moral illiteracy.

The thoughts they engender
Will soon create a mind
Full of unethical nonsense
A disgrace to humankind.

When life is sorely cheapened
By influence so crude
Then will Man's baser feelings
All finer thoughts exclude.

How does Man attain
A mind of quiet peace
If all his thoughts are lowly?
Will there be another lease,

Another chance be given
To prove he can succeed
In growing wise inspirit
Not bowing down to greed?

Or will our God
Despairingly descend
Upon a world so wicked
And bring it to an end?

Eric Allday

1986 VILLAGE CHRISTMAS PREPARATION - CHORLEY, STAFFS

As we prepare for Christmas, with shopping, lights, trees and gifts,
Let us remember, lest we forget, to prepare for the greatest gift of all,
The 'Birth of Jesus,' God's son, with whom Christianity began.
In a village not far from town, when winter begins to show her crown,
With frosty lanes and icy winds, villagers meet
Wrapped up against the cold, scarves, hats, gloves and boots.
As down the lanes we descend, lights, lanterns at the ready,
Carol sheets in hand, as carolling we go.
We all enjoy this yearly singing, young, old and not so young,
Vicar at the helm, just to encourage us, voices raised.
Lovely, sweet and some not so sweet, but willing hearts.
The wind doth blow, but on we go down winding lanes, past brook
and farm,
Knocking doors, any requests, we will do our best.
Mince pies and sherry sometimes offered,
But that can wait until last.
Our voices raised in adoration
As we herald Christmas morn, when the Saviour of the world was born.
By now our voices, wearing thin,
As the effects of the frosty air begin to show
But ever willing on we go, our collection seems to begin to grow,
The church funds will profit, we know.
As from the lanes we emerge, the lights of the village are in view,
We know there's a roaring fire in the village pub, so, up we trek and
onward go.
The pub is bright with tree and lights, cosy, warm, welcoming,
in we go.
It is all worthwhile, this carol singing, they pass around a collection box
Drinkers, one and all, join us with 'Silent Night.'

We wave goodbye and homeward go, our last preparation is complete,
Some may have weary feet, but that's what preparing for Christmas
is all about.
Next year, they'll be there again I have no doubt. God bless carollers
One and all, 'Oh Come All Ye Faithful' on Christmas morn.

Irene G Corbett

WILD IN THE SKY

There is a beginning
born from an egg like an orange-brown cratered moon
growing adult with dark cliff back and wave white under body.

There is a magnet
that will draw down an osprey from its flight path,
returning on a wing, as warrior flier comes home to base.

It is the pull
of a warm wriggling pair of scraggy chicks, barely feathered,
which become jump jets, pathfinders, white-tailed pilot hunters.

There is a hunger
ever present making them peck seaweed, twigs, stones, each other.
Food for survival means muscle to ride windborne, wild in the sky.

It is hunting
Blood-surging desire which turns sharp their sea-hawk eyes,
nest staring at fish bones, herring scales and mollusc shells.

There is a splash
a leg action entry, bill aided from stretched, taloned feet
on long, slender white legs – almost jodhpurs with spurs.

It is the strike
the caught fish is held fast, pinned in a vice hold, is trapped
then aligned for the return flight to two gorging chicks.

There is a sudden shade
a fast, Y-shadow above the cowering brood makes them crouch,
a dark wingspan's eclipse, young bills gape for feeding.

It is the hen bird
her roughened pad feet grip a headless, slippery sand-dab,
her hooked bill rips strips to their upward held gullets.

There is survival
the lee of a crevice gives shelter from arrowhead winds,
kinder winters, charitable hearts lift ospreys to sky's freedom.

Dennis Marshall

STAND

Who crusades with love, whose cause peace,
They are the freedom fighters, the voices who speak for
Those silent heroes . . .
Those whose faces, smiles, hearts and minds,
Dreams, joys, experiences and loves,
Chances, choices become so many stilled,
Silent lost lives and voices . . .
For them we stand.
Our cause hope, not violence, vengeance, lies, death,
For sons, daughters, sisters, brothers, fathers, mothers.
We honour the memories of all victims in seeking a better way,
For the living history, made now, will stand and mark killers
Not as liberators, but as the deluded, dark, pathetic cowards
Their own actions make them.
For the children learn – from history earn,
For the will of love wrought, against the wrath of war fought.
Lay down the rage of fears,
The long rain of tears.
Face without guns, come together in peace, bring the years.
Now, tears only of joy, to share,
Release in freedom. Stand . . .
For the future's our care!

Paul Holland

TIME

Time waits for no one
No matter who you may be
Make the most of the time you have
Fill it with worthwhile things
For time is so precious
And not to be wasted
For you do not know what time you have
The less you have
The more you want,
The more you need
Time flies by on silent wings
And, before you know it
Time has gone
Forever.

The hands on the clock tick away the seconds
That make up the minutes
That make up the hours
That make up the days
That make up the weeks
That make up the months
That make up the years
Of Life.

Vanessa Bell

PARADISE
(Dedicated to those who tend Mill Gardens)

I know a lovely, quite place,
Where my troubled mind finds peace.
Where beauty lurks in every space,
Amazing wonders never cease.

Healing when I enter there,
Embraces me like warm, soft winds.
Glorious colours, naught can compare,
Where little birds can spread their wings.

The Avon flows past my side,
Nearby the ruins of an ancient bridge
Tell tales of days gone by with pride,
The old mill wheel there used to ride.

Swans nest and rear their pretty young,
Serene and calm they gently glide.
Their home is warm with rushes hung,
Safe from all the night they hide.

Secret pathways going nowhere,
But oh the joy of getting there.
Gentle lawns curve round the flowers,
The joy of life doth me ensnare.

The castle with its mighty tower,
Guards every creature in its lair.
Loved and safe through every hour,
In Warwick's lovely garden fair.

Betty Smyth

THE QUEST FOR THE ANSWER

Silence is a sharp, foreboding cry, shattering the morn.
Splinters of wild red light, another birth is brutally born.
This new life must follow to make the cycle complete,
For the mother creator makes life out of heat.

As steps turn into runs and our eyes behold
The beauty of nature, wonders of old,
Forced to make waves in our innocent years,
Holding light to our treasures, banishing our fears.

As time gallops onwards like a wondrous steed,
We're dragging on behind to make way for a new seed.
So what is the reason, where is the truth?
Each minute spent thinking is a minute of youth.

The moon appears pale as milk
And turns to blood in a sky of silk.
Our minds start to wonder, our hearts question why
Does this beauty so awesome live on, while we die?

As the tranquil mood ebbed, twilight leaped into tune.
Sky and sun blessed the evening moon.
Hundreds of years reflect on rebel oak trees,
Only the breath of life can bring us to our knees.

Do our minds carry on thought, in the dark passages of sight.
A turmoil never-ending, a tunnel of light.
No answer for ever, never at rest,
Or is death the beginning of the end of our quest?

D Hughes

THE PRESENT PROBLEM

The present is that fine moving line
Moving from past into future time
It has no dimension of any kind
No fixed location but in the mind

Is the present our ability to grasp
A little of the future with the past?
Memory and prescience anticipation
A subjective awareness situation

When we are happy that line moves too fast
If only the present could longer last
When we are unhappy it moves too slow
As only too well do we all know

Because the present is that fine moving line
Where past and future are hard to define
Another question will come to mind
Just what is this thing that we call time?

K W Benoy

SEVEN SEASONS

Frost came in the night, it stole my world
Over mountain tops a strange mist curled
Images of nature, once so pristinely true
Were lost in a landscape, cold, frosty, blue.
So tell me not mournful, seasons of thy numbers
Our souls are dead where pollution slumbers
For our lives are but an empty dream
And thins are never what they seem.
The wind of change has no soul
For earth destruction's become her goal.
There is a reaper, his name is death
He stalks our world with destructive breath.
Trees and flowers where they grow between
In the twenty-first century are no longer seen.
There is no light on earth or in heaven
As angels of the night bring season seven
And where tall oak trees' branches stand
Comes the cruellest sea to cover our land.
Nature's cold, damp touch, forbidding, aspired
Bringing misty fogs and raging forest fires,
The winds and snows bring melted flood,
Stormy rain clouds send trains of mud.
Nature arches her back, she screams with pain
Calling season seven to wax and wane.
Ice age is coming, Mother Earth dims her lights,
Our world's cold and barren, without nights.
Nature sends her wrath, world's immortal fears
Globes covered by darkness embrace apocalyptic years.

Ann Hathaway

A PERFECT HOLIDAY

A perfect holiday just for me,
Things to do and lots to see.
I know where to go! I'll go to Egypt,
To see the pyramids and exotic beaches.

The palm trees and statues I'll see all day,
And upon the dunes of sand I'll lay.
The sun sits up high,
It lights up the day.

By the looks of it, I'll have a nice holiday!

Archana Kapoor

WALCOT STREET

The narrow street was crowded.
A freedom pervaded the air.
Everyone appeared relaxed and happy.
A procession wound its way down the cobbled street.
Here drums were beating, the rhythm vibrated into every being.
Each individual in the troupe moved in unison.
Bohemians young and old alike radiated love to the onlookers.
Children beneath the multicoloured paper dragon undulated
and swayed to the flow of music.
All my senses were intense:
I would have loved to join the procession and danced.
The length of the street had come alive with sounds.
The sun too added warmth and reflected colour.
Stalls were aglow with sparkling jewellery.
Taste buds were tempted as the aroma of barbecued food
permeated the air,
My attention was drawn to a young woman, arm in arm
with her grandmother.
Curiously I watched.
How lovely they were together, how supportive.
Each no doubt having full admiration for the other.
The young woman possibly in her early twenties moved slowly
and gently.
Her head was shaven, a small tattoo peeped from behind her right ear.
Her long, striped, rainbow gown hid her body,
only an ankle showed above her black and white striped mules.
I admired her.
What courage at such a young age,
so self-assured, confident and at ease with her persona.
I ask myself,
'Why do I conform?'
Perhaps I'm afraid, too old and set in my ways to change.
'Am I?'
No, not yet.

Audrey Faulkner O'Connor

NOT LOVE THEN

Not love then, friendship only:
So we decreed and so it comes about –
One row, one misery-bout
Too many
Ends our life together.
Begins the task of disengagement now,
And we must ponder how
To sever
The bonds our years have wrought –
How to unpick the complicated knot
That bound us head and heart.
We court
A civilised stance, yet
Know that love's a savage thing when soured
And what we would desire
May not
Be ours to have - (where love
Is sovereign reason has no argument) -
And fickle good intent
May prove –
But enough:
What follows must we be steeled
To bear for, like an infection stubborn to yield,
Love takes some killing off.

Philip Sanders

LOOKING

I've been looking for a long time now,
Searching for a spirit, known as God.
Maybe He's in the shape of a golden flower,
Or in a majestic tree.
Can I praise in word or song
Steadfast and strong,
Searching for so long, for the spirit known as God.
Maybe He's in clouds of brilliant blue.

Or maybe He's in me and you,
Longing to appear in deeds of kindness.
I've been looking for a long time now.

Donovan Powell

CHIMNEYS

Up and up, right to the sky,
Brick on brick,
      the layers lie.
Far down beneath the engines turned,
That powered the mills
      to keep the towns.

On manor houses
      they twist and twist,
An earthen red, of Tudor brick.
Winters were so warm,
      the hearth beside,
As many of them complement,
      two by two, side by side.

Off a building,
      long since gone,
Now so serene in a garden
      both do dwell,
No smoke does blacken,
      no wind does chide,
So majestic stands the king
With his gracious queen
      by his side.

From a palace to a crofter's dwell,
Smoke rises through them,
      from hearth to heaven,
A peaceful place to abide,
Through the windows, fires glow,
Full of warmth and love inside.

Patricia Westwood

I WOKE

Last night I woke to the sounds of
an angel screaming
the shattering of a dream
the loss of your gentle breathing
and fierce devotion

Last night I woke to the sounds of
a child's dream whimper
turn and toss
the filling of a void with memories.

On the last night you woke, you turned
brushed away the tears.
The dying in your breasts
Forgotten for a brief moment.

Last night I woke to the sounds of
memories
in drowned silence.

Elwyn Jones

BATTLE OF WITS?

Said my mother to my father,
'I know you'd *like* to shirk
but you're always doing some thing
that gives *me* much more work.'

Said my father to my mother,
'That simply is not true;
but I would be doing nothing
if work wasn't made by *you.*'

Said my mother to my father,
'I can't do nowt all day
cos *I'm* the one who does the work
that you don't do: anyway,
if I'm doing nothing
I can't make work for you –
you must do it all yourself.'
Said Father, 'Yes, I do.'

David Thomsett Palmer

ON THE NATIVITY

The soul which forged the secrets of the sky,
Is conscious of His mother's face, of light
Upon the swarthy peasants' hands and night,
Which muffles every mortal sound and sigh
And now that love which brought Him from on high
Is kindled by a mere caress and sight
Of silken hair and hay and lanterns bright
With dancing flame.
O happy shepherds in your humble bliss
And kings who found an end to pilgrimage,
For on the threshold certain strangers stand,
Way-worn, besmurched with sin,
Reflecting this to be the author of the winter's rage
And bitter journeys in a barren land

Ann Bradley

NEIGHBOURS' KIDS

You've heard of the programme, 'Neighbours from Hell',
Well I can relate to that as well.
I love my garden, but when I go out,
The kids over the fence give me a shout.
'Give us our ball,' it's always the same,
But as soon as I do, it's back again.
They break the fence and trample the flowers,
The litter comes over to me in showers.
Their parents don't care, just sit in the chair,
The windows wide open, the music a-blare.
Should I think of a way of getting them back,
Draw up a plan, then make an attack,
Or should I just try and keep my cool,
'Cause I think next week they'll be back at school?

Elizabeth Bourne

SUMMER

The sun shines brightly in the ocean-blue sky,
As a happy cloud went sailing by,
I looked up at a majestic oak tree
And it smiled back down at me.
I saw a flower by the road,
Nearby, a stream gently flowed.
The day is beautiful when I'm awake,
As I gazed upon the waters of the mirror-calm lake,
Water spouted joyfully from a fountain,
In the distance stood a snow-capped mountain,
The sun smiled throughout the day
In the merry month of May,
A bird flew up on high,
Then another passed on by,
The grass is so green and the sky is so blue,
While I walk along, another sunset is due,
I like the sun when it does shine,
I only wish it could be mine,
A cheerful bird sang a song
For a mate that won't be long,
As butterfly floated silently past,
And I wondered how long summer would last.

K Delaney

DREAMS

In the twilight of my hours,
In the midnight of my room,
Darkness comes around me,
Night-time comes too soon,

Sunlight wants to open,
Everything that's closed,
Paths that need exploring,
The ones I never chose.

Take me on that journey,
To where I could have been,
The richness of the knowledge,
Of what I could have seen,

For now I stop and ponder,
For wanting of the past,
Of pathways that I'd alter,
Aspirations that I'd cast,

My journey is not over,
My midnight's not arrived,
I have the power to change things,
Do more than just survive.

Lisa Dean

THE SYMPHONY OF CHIMES

Rhyming out the hours from atop his chiming towers,
Old Father Time has tolled ever since being born;
However many has he told the time to from dusk till dawn?
Booming with a voice of brass and clockwork, then and now as
Second, minute, hour, day, week, month, year
Go ringing overhead bringing tomorrow to our doors.
Time flinging out his seeds, sowing on the shores
Of the waters that course like a flowing elixir,
High across the sleeping villages, towns, cities;
Spillages of time flood upon our dreaming heads,
Streaming into our rooms to wash away our beds
On a river of forever, into the abyss.
Sounding every quarter for each daughter and son,
Time peals away the layers of their lives, till he tolls
His final knell, and the bells like a billion souls
Sing aloud their symphony of chimes in unison.

Jonathan Goodwin

I COULD BE

I could be the wind that sails
On a choppy sea,
Or a grub-ridden russet
That falls from a tree.
I could be snow on a mountain slope
For climbers to tread,
Or a book in a library,
Virgin, not read.
I could be curls on a forehead,
Golden and fair,
Or a flying trapeze artist,
That if I dare.
I could be rubies, pearls
And gold if I must,
Though precious they be,
I'd be pans of gold dust.

Joan Margaret Clemmow

EVENSONG

Night's curtain falls
on sunset's ocean stage,
and dying day's last scene.

Bright harbour lights
turn heaving, oily waters
into liquid gold.

Mist forms eerily,
spiralling like spectral smoke
from long-dead fires.

Soon satellites rise,
seeming glowing sparks
ascending heavenwards.

David Hancock

SUNRISE IN MY GARDEN

Crimson sky above
Emerald grass
Dewdrops, glass shimmering
Soon they would disappear into the
Misty morning sky

Swaying with the light breeze are
The upright, chunky pine trees
A dim golden light shines through
The windows of our house,
Casting a lemon glow on the furniture.

The air smells as fresh as fresh fruit
And the sounds are of nothing at all
At last the citrus, orange sun peaks
Through the clouds
And into the crimson to azure sky.

Ciara Foley (12)

TIME PASSES BY

How I would love
Someone to care
Passing time sitting
On the deckchair
The summer is ending
Everyone is going home
I live by the sea
Passing time is a hobby
For me
I look across to see
Who is left
Passing time is the best
When everyone goes home
I am left on my own
Just passing time.

P Wardle

SAVIOURS

Tumbling down from heaven the
saints are seeking out those
who feel lost and alone.
Scattering gifts of faith and hope,
amongst the poor and forgotten.

The child who prays the footsteps
in the night, won't stop outside
her bedroom door.
The battered wife who's packed her cases
so many times, but never yet found the
courage to leave.
Animals abused in the name of science,
pets that are knocked about really don't
understand what they're doing wrong.
Baby seals slaughtered for their pure
white coats, now tainted with blood
of man's greed.

Peals of thunder signal God's anger,
lightning, the pain he feels.
Where did he go wrong with his children?
He didn't intend us to be this way.
A beautiful silver rain will fall from
the dark sky and wash our land clean again.

Vicky Stevens

ULTIMATE SACRIFICE

As a babe in arms he lay
Showing his baby charms that day
Who knew then what he would do
Give his life for me and you
While on earth he preached and taught
Then on the cross at Calvary our freedom he bought
Now from our Lord above
Around us we have his arms of love
Now all I have to say
Is get down on your knees and pray
And ask him into your life today.

Claire Robinson

YOUR HEART OR YOUR LIFE!

Hiding in the shadows,
Heart Bandit, Passion Swindler,
You caught me by surprise.

The kiss you dealt was lethal – knocked me off my feet,
So I handed it over.
(It wasn't an idle threat.)

Please Mr Robber, think about the trauma you've caused.
Starlight in my eyes, a dopey, foolish grin,
The feeling that I never want to be separated from you.
Don't smirk! This is a serious crime.

One vicious account of love burglary, stolen from a smitten woman
Has the minimum sentence of unconditional love for all eternity,
And this is clearly a serious case.

So,
Better go on the run love thief,
'Cause if I catch you, you'll know about it!

Jeanette Bruckshaw

SWEET MEMORIES

I remember the day we first said, 'Hello',
A boy tugged my hair and would not let go.
You told him to stop it or you'd flay him alive,
You a strong eight-year old,
Me a wee five.

I remember the time we first fell in love.
The stars were shining, the moon high above.
You held me quite tightly and whispered my name,
You kissed me so sweetly, my heart was aflame.
As I said, 'I love you,' you kissed me again.

Then came our wedding day,
When we both said, 'I will,'
Our families were side by side
In the church on the hill.
The choirboys sang the hymns so in style.
'A vision in white,' you said
As I walked down the aisle.

Our family increased as the years carried on,
First a sweet daughter, then a wee son.
And now we are waiting for news to arrive,
Of a new addition, our first grandchild.

E Timmins

AN OLD BOOK

The smell of an old book,
Its musty, layered dust,
You love to breathe and
Touch its tattered corner leaves,
With brown marks smudged,
Snags and tears, spills and nicks,
The body, it presents, spine stiff,
With yearly pride that it has lived
To see three score and ten,
The confidante you visit
When Time is not your friend.

Emma-Louise Cartwright

THE CHANTRESS IN THE EGYPTIAN TEMPLE

The golden orb of Ra greets the new day on the horizon,
As at the banks of the Nile,
The temple priestesses stand poised, ready to indulge in the water,
Playfully in quick succession they venture in,
Filling their pitchers to the brim,
Taking it in turns to pour the streaming water over their naked bodies,
This ritualistic cleansing for purity a necessary part of their regime,
For they were to administer to the gods,
Back inside the temple, concealed from the light of day,
They made their way across the silver inlaid floor.

Past the intricately carved columns and where walls set
                                        with lapis lazuli,
Replicated the midnight firmament,
On reaching their quarters they clad themselves in fine white robes,
Placed fringed, long hairpiece upon their shaven heads,
And adorned their necks and foreheads,
With the blue lotus flower and its fragrant perfume,
Assembling together the requisites required,
For their first visit of the day before the idol, set within its abode,
On golden trays they placed fruit, bread and sweetmeats,
Soaking the blue lotus in carafes of the finest wine.

Fine linen clothes for the god placed across their shoulders,
With candles alight slowly in procession they moved,
Chanting in repetition a variety of notes,
Before the idol they danced energetically,
Performing back-bends and back-flips,
In this the first of three visits,
They then moved forward to the next idol,
As the day neared its close, they retired to their own chamber,
Satisfied that they had placated the gods,
Knowing that Ra would rise another day.

Ann G Wallace

NATIVITY

One Christmas at St Lukes,
vandals broke in and stole all the figures
from the nativity scene. (The image
of glue-sniffers or opportunists trying to barter
with pawnbrokers for plastic Wise Men still amuses.)

Rather than suffer the disappointment
of an empty manger and a ghost town stable,
the children of the congregation decided
to provide their own replacements.

That year, Joseph was an Action Man,
Mary - a Barbie doll.
The menagerie surrounding the infant child
included a My Little Pony, two Beanie Bears,
Tigger and a fluffy pig.
The old ladies knitted shepherds
and the three Wise Men
were, in fact, Tinky Winky, La La and Po.

Jesus was lovingly recreated from plasticine
and placed in a box of extra long matches.

Ask anyone which Christmas they remember most
and they'll tell you - it was the one
where everyone pulled together; where the church
felt alive again; where a star settled overhead
and led the Teletubbies to Cradley Heath.

Andrew Detheridge

ALMOST A STORM

Have you ever looked at a painting for so long
You feel as if you are on the inside looking out?
I see a painting of a beach,
A lone fisherman tries to get his boat to shore
Before the weather changes.
As the storm approaches, the darkening skies above him
Grow blacker by the minute.
My thoughts begin to grow darker too.
A wave of depression sweeps over me.
The air around me feels oppressive.
My head is throbbing, vision slightly blurred.
Slowly the menacing skies get lighter.
As the storm passes over, my head starts to clear.
And I am on the outside once again looking in.

Adrianne Jones

POPPIES

A wonderful expanse of countryside
Not so far from the town
Driving along a road
Views of grassy banks sloping down
With rows of scarlet poppies
Heads high towards the light
Reminiscent of Flanders fields
Men's buttoned uniforms, shining bright
Poppy heads waving in the gentle breeze
Soldiers called to attention – with ease
Waiting for a signal
The command to move on
The poppies still remain
Even though the men have gone.

Katherine Parker

LOVE KNOWS NO BOUNDS

Love knows no distance
And certainly no age
Love knows no evil
And is not content with rage.

Love is always patient
Tries always to be kind
Love is never controlling
Yet it is hard to find.

Love should be forever
Eternal, it should be
Always in your heart
Awaiting patiently.

Love should have no bounds
Try not to tie it down
You are what you are
Love doesn't make you frown.

Love is more than words
For actions speak aloud
That's why love stands out
When you're in a crowd.

Love is understanding
Gentle to one's soul
Love makes life compete
That's always been my goal.

Love is all around us
And it's here to stay
Sometimes it may hurt
A small price one has to pay.

Lee D Jones

THE BLUE LADY

She arrived in leg-warmers and trainers
She changed into a blue dress with high heels
There was the faded elegance of a charity shop
In her demeanour and white hair

She ordered a crepe with strawberries and tea
She observed the comings and goings
With the eyes of a fledgling child

She told me she was a poet of 150 times
200 if you included 50 by the paranormal soul above
She told me food was an art form

She said she was very creative and artistic
Most would have passed her by
As an eccentric lady

But within the voice that told me
Her clothes come from Birmingham and Wales
I heard the cry of the child within
Who was lost and searching for herself

Seeking the youth lost and love abandoned
Within the bright lights of restaurants and nightclubs
The need to speak to anyone who would listen
To the loneliness of the soul

I heard that voice
And the sorrow of its pain

Carol Bradford

FRIEND OR FOE

I think that Mother Nature, to females, is unfair,
For look and see how many man have lovely, curly hair,
Eyelashes, long and silky
Flutter on their cheek
And they don't have any problems
With their simple physique.
And look as we get older, the tortures women have to bear,
With dropping this and spreading that . . .
It's really most unfair.

On men, grey hairs distinguished,
On women . . . old age is setting in.

And laughter lines on men,
On women are a sin.
No hot flushes for the male,
Or drying-out of skin.
They get a second chance, it seems,
We don't get a look in.
Now think of Mother Nature,
Imagine if you can . . .
Don't you think it possible,
Mother Nature is a . . . man.

Jacqueline Claire Davies

HE WONDERS WHAT'S THERE

As nature unfolds the grey mist dawns,
the starlings' song all forlorn.
He walks along, head held down,
the world on his shoulders
shown in his heartbroken frown.

All too much for any to bear,
he looks into the water and
wonders what's there.
Would anyone miss him, would anyone care?
It's all too much for him to bear.
He loved her dearly, till death do us part,
it's all too much for one's tender heart.

Can he go on, or should he try,
would it be betrayal or would she forgive?
Their love was so great, wondrous and true,
is crying all that he can do?
His grief is so hard, so murderous to bear,
he loved her so much, he wonders what's there.

Is life worth living, to have loved but lost,
or is it worth finding out to our bitter cost?
He looks into the stillness and wonders if there's anything there.
Is there a beyond? Will he ever see her smile again,
or is it his fate, to hold a brick as a heart,
for he has lost his best mate.
As he walks along he wonders what's there,
will he ever meet his true love again,
or is life just too unfair?

M Taylor

THE UNFORTUNATE FORTUNATE

Did you see the destitute on the box,
Men in posh suits and women in posh frocks,
Expecting to convince someone like me
That they are poor and live in poverty?

I don't know, they seem so genuine too,
In our day they would have been well-to-do,
To exist like us, they wouldn't know how,
It was hard for us then, not hard like now.

Their kids in trainers and designer jeans,
Probably don't know what poverty means,
They look well-nourished and not under fed,
I doubt they ever slept four in a bed.

The trouble with them, they think they are poor,
We could never keep the wolf from our door,
Not us raggy-arsed kids, with worn-out boots,
Who thought that the rich were the ones in suits.

Peter Chaney

MOTHER

A friend, a sister and a mother
all three rolled into one.
That is what she is to me
this woman I call my mum.

I have been richly blessed
by her care and love
which she daily shares with me.
Her patience and understanding
is given so generously.

In my prayers I give God thanks
for the way He has planned our lives.
For no one else could ever have known
the price of her sacrifice.

She has given up her life for me
her dreams and ambitions put aside,
to concentrate on her daughter
for whom she does provide.

My words and acts of thanks and praise
seem little in repay,
for the wondrous mother she has been to me
throughout each and every day.

Natasha Jackson

MOTHER OF MINE

Just sitting here in silence,
With thoughts of years gone by,
Remembering my mother,
How she always made us try.

Each morning with her special smile,
She would do each little chore,
Make the breakfast, wash the dishes, clean the floor,
Just like she'd done before.

It's very true there is no other
Can take the place of your dear mother.
The day you find this is true,
When the Lord God Almighty takes her from you.

This day you will remember,
When you're left all alone,
The best friend in the whole wide world
Gone to her heavenly home.

Fond memories will always stay
Of my mother, sound and true,
No other friend in all this world
Will be as true to you.

Heavenly Father up above,
Give my mother a great, big hug.
Inside my heart she'll always stay,
Till we meet again on our special day.

Carolann Elsmore

QUALITY OF LIFE

Where is the quality
Give me my sanity
I've done no wrong
I just want to be mentally strong
Everything I seem to do
Just turns out like I haven't got a clue
Please free me of the pain
Oh Lord it's such a strain
Physically everything looks alright
But inside I'm not so bright
Rid me of this state of mind
The world is so cruel, why can't it be more kind?
I wish others would understand
That when I don't feel so grand
I'm not too good on communication
Never mind the welfare of the nation
Everyone has their needs
Just like farmers sowing their seeds
I'd love to reap the harvest of good health
Then I'd say I have a lot of wealth
Hear my prayer almighty God above
Bless me with your tender care and love
When you appear on this earth again oh Lord
No one will have time to be looking bored
Those of us who know you will rejoice
Those who don't, have to make a choice
The heavenly Father is near
Too late to shed a tear.

Denise Walters

THE SANDS OF TIME

A man looks up to a heaven he no longer believes in
As jagged lightning spears a dark, delirious sky.
Pregnant clouds about to give birth to acid rain
Roll ominously over satanic hills.
He shakes his head in sorrow,
As icy tears roll down a face ravaged by life.
The sound of thunder echoes across a river swollen to distortion.
'It's coming,' he remarks to an empty abyss of a once vibrant world.
The sands of time are running out faster than his tomorrows
The river turns crimson.
The man looks on in horror as his dreams slowly die
Like moths caught in an eternal flame.
Armageddon has arrived.

Jacky Stevens

THE CONSERVATORY

Conservatory or Observatory, what is this place
For thinking, meeting, work or leisure space
Built to extend and also conserve
The sunshine's warmth and nature's verve.

Conservatory or Conservatoire
Where strains of music rend the air
Or for Elocution, the spoken word
With splendid diction can be heard
To perfect performance for public view
Of a talent or skill presented anew.

Conservatory is a place where plants
Respond to warmth with growth enhanced
Greenhouse effects capture those sunny days
Except for ozone holes and harmful rays.

Conserve is to keep from change, to maintain
So the best of nature should remain
Conservation, environment, trees and open spaces
Free from roads, railways and superstore-type places.

Conservatory conversation will be broad
Conservative only if one is bored
Occasional music and sometimes snores
Both inside, yet out of doors.

John Fairhurst

MELTING DOWN THE IRON LADY

It was thought that she could only melt in hell,
But she began to melt when Heseltine did rebel.
Yes, she who gave a knighthood to the man who forge-mastered
                                              her hair
And destroyed forever the meanings of words: thrift, trust, truth
                                              and care.
Who emasculated the unions and waged vendetta 'gainst author
                                    of 'Spycatcher' (MI)
And left infirm, unemployed, homeless, disabled and elderly only their
                                    eyes with which to cry.
Who saw the sentencing of Sarah Tisdel – a Whitehall 'mole,'
And the BBC invaded by Secret Service which documents relating
                                    to Zercon satellite, stole.
Who set dad against son, brother against brother, uncle against nephew
                                    in the mining communities,
During and beyond the miners' strike which saw her private army
                                    and mounties.
Who made union workers at GCHQ scapegoats for royal Diana's
                                    messages intercepting,
And 'worshipped' and 'idol' to Salmon Rushdie whom Islam
                                    was insulting.
Who 'squeezed every drop of blood' from ordinary, law-abiding,
                                    decent folk,
By 'clamping around their necks the poll tax yoke'.
So melt Iron Lady, melt into your funeral crucible,
You, who believed that a heart of iron, would make you invincible.

R Wiltshire

TRUE LOVE REVEALED

True love revealed
Salvation's plan sealed
In a child of whose birth
Few realised his worth
Yet poor humble shepherds
Heard the angelic words
A Saviour is born
In a stable at dawn
Christ the Lord is his title
To see him is vital
So leaving their sheep
And losing their sleep
They rushed down the hillside
To kneel at his bedside
In a cattle stall
Lay the creator of all
Oh wonder of wonders
Such a sight they did ponder
Have you ever wondered why
Though two thousand years have gone by
That millions of people
In churches with steeples
And chapels and halls
Answer the altar call
To follow this one
Born in ages gone
For that child was God's Son
Revealed as the one
Who came to show a lost world
God's great love unfurled

Rebecca Walker

WAITING FOR THE UNKNOWN

Waiting for the unknown
I cry myself to sleep.
Thinking of you only
for the dreams are mine
to keep.

Waiting for the unknown
you give your heart to me.
Lead me to the future
for the past I have seen.

Waiting for the unknown
I sit and wait for you.
Do I follow my dreams
that I know inside
my heart are true?

E M Hyde

THE PATH TO HAPPINESS

The mind is like an autumn leaf,
hanging on a tree.
It only takes a gentle breeze
to blow and set it free.

Free to wander aimlessly
down paths that are unknown,
trying hard to make some sense
of where it next should roam.

At first this proves impossible,
as the paths all look the same,
for you never seem to see the sun,
that guides you, just the rain.

You fear the many obstacles
laid out along the way.
But, gradually the path grows clear,
and the sky turns blue not grey.

Then there in front's the opening
that you've been searching for,
the one that leads to laughter
and happiness once more.

Yvonne York

THE MASK

I am made to frighten you
To frighten you
I've been to Hollywood
Pinewood too
I've been to Los Angeles
London too

You may have seen me frightening you
Without really knowing it was me
Yes, I was in the evil gardener
Amongst many a film

Many a play too
On Broadway and the West End

I've been worn by many a star
Boris Karloff, Vincent Price, Peter Cushing
To name but many

Some have refused to wear me -
Too frightening was said

Now in semi-retirement
On the wall of the living room
Of my owner
Still frightening people
Who come to the house

I often wonder
Shall I fall off the wall
In the night
And give my owner a fright?

Then I think no
I'm happy and content
Here on the wall

David J Hall

THE RAFT RACE

We go to Deeping
(That's called St James),
For summer raft races,
Even if it rains.

Last year was brilliant,
The weather was hot,
And with plenty of watering holes
Between these we could hop.

This year was wet,
The River Welland banks slippy,
So to get round the weir
Was a might tricky.

With rafts back in the river,
On the bridge we were waiting,
To dredge them with flour;
(It's tradition at Deeping).

Some rafters fought back:
They sent water jets high,
Which we tried to evade,
But got caught, oh my!

It's such good fun though,
And in a good cause,
We hope it continues
For years and years.

Mary McPhee

ODE TO THE GRANGE

Arlington, Morfa and Hewell Grange
Sixty plus engines of the mid power range,
Designed by Collett to follow the Star
All over the South West she travelled afar.
Pulling coaches or freight, she took her turn
Good South Wales coal, her firebox did burn,
Her duties were varied, no task too small
This class of engine stood proud, so tall.
The banking rotas were second to none
In the blink of an eye, and then she was gone,
Rain, sleet or snow, in glorious sun
The crews were happy when their shift was done.

For thirty odd years she did her job
When the end came, many people did sob,
Made redundant and sent to the yard
For many enthusiasts they found it hard.
That none of your class would ever live on
Your memory still lingers although you're gone,
Only in pictures can we see you in your glory
They alone now tell the story.
Of a proud class of engine, beloved by all
Why, oh why, did you have to fall?
So raise a glass to one of Swindon's best
May your ghost be laid to rest.

Joe Griffiths

THE PAINTER

In a corner, in a dormer tucked away
Beneath an opal starlit plate,
Aslant, aslope, in rooftop silhouette askew
All purple-blue of slate . . .
Where pinnacle of Iron Tower
Marks the twilight midnight hour . . . here,
Held within one cobweb-circle window's fate
Concentric, fat and round and 'dangle-down',
Spiders twang, all in a game,
Like onions on a bicycle frame . . .
Far above the cobble street
The painter's life is sweet and free . . .
Though . . . (arriére-pensée) . . .
This 'affaire de coeur' still, as yet . . . is,
Incomplete.
So fierce the consecration here
As concentration's hues collide
To mix and melt, to fantasize and straight
The dark and lengthy look . . .
With palm is pulled aside.
At frowning tilt, a self-scolded head now,
Once again begins the 'pas de deux' of yes and no,
That 'dance' behind the brow.
Between his teeth a paintbrush gripped and
On the floor a canvas, ripped.
Forthwith!
The mystic hands advance to form a digit-frame
Through which . . . he weasel peers . . . as if
From out a weaver's mind.
Soft waterfall of silk falls out, crimson,
Light in shade,
The sheen of which excites the mind
As if in heaven, made to clothe his Mademoiselle
Reclining there, a facile nude who, finger licks

And frivolous at chocolate picks, within a box . . .
The evening through . . . 'pari passu'.
Again the dualism starts.
On canvas new . . . now makes his mark,
Inspiring up a thousand lark, which . . .
Bluster-out, in twilight park,
To flock about that mind absurd,
Whilst landlord, snide, at a lower floor,
Pimps rent, invigilate . . . from a secret whore.
Askance . . . at portiére observes the painter this,
Then forwards the all important brushy swerves
Which . . . for all the hours soon,
Will swing about the 'gas lamp moon'
Full at his height,
Painting shadows round the night.

Roger Mosedale

JUST STRANGE?

I had a dream that everything was calm,
Everybody smiled and asked how you are.
But then everybody turned around
And frowned and laughed at me,
Saying that I'm dirty and I dress horribly.

I cry and cry till my eyes are sore,
That dream was real, I am so sure.
It looked and felt like it happened,
But of course it couldn't be,
Or is that maybe I can see.

I can see the future in my head,
Now the future I will dread.
People turn evil, every single one.
Unless everybody tries to change,
Or maybe this dream was just strange.

Leila Rujas-Gill (12)

RUTH'S RETURN

Sometime where milk-white moonbeams melt,
You came, soft as a shadow, you came;
And your soothing fingers crept
About my hair
And upon my face.
With promises untold of firesides and blue peace
At the yellow bar of ebbing light;
With my child's mouth at your breast,
And strangely still
Long you stayed
Your hair cascading over my face,
Fair as flowered June
It bound my sleep,
The silence was rich and deep
And mystic as the dreaming moon.
Long you stayed
Until the dawn tremored in the hills,
Ivory curtains shook and sighed
Then you fled, soft upon the moonlight
Back to the dead,
Suddenly it was cold, grey and dim
There was a moaning on the wind
And I was alone, alone.

Sean Conway

THE KISS

Nathan kissed me - so tenderly.
It warmed my heart, like sunrise
On a shimmering sea.
'Again!' he whispered softly.

Nathan kissed me - such a loving kiss.
It lingered, like the morning dew, upon my lips.
'Again!' I heard him say.

Nathan kissed me - a heartfelt, precious kiss.
Would that each new day could be as beautiful as this.
'Again!' softly I whispered.

Marie P Holbeche

WHISPERS IN THE WIND

Have you not heard their voices?
Do you listen to the voices on the wind?
Do you not hear the plaintive calling -
Not hear or see the underlying currents
Or the channels of their mind?
Have you not read the signs
And the symptoms all around?
Now you hear the blast, a terrible
    great sound,
The sound of a disaster as towers
    topple to the ground.
Where is God? Who has done this?
Did you not hear the whisperings
    on the wind?
Someone must pay, let us bomb them
    into the ground.
'Give us bread, give us water'
    was all they had said -
In the whisperings in the wind,
Listen and you'll hear what
    they said
'All we want is bread!
Bread not bombs.'
The war should be on want instead!
No one heard the whispering
    in the wind -
As the cymbals clash in a mighty
    orchestral sound.
But the whispering goes unheard.
The status symbol in the stratosphere,
Has now become the instrument
    of fear.
Now is the time for all to shed a tear
And listen to the whispering in our ear!

Patricia Arnett

MEETING THE ALIENS

The aliens came last year,
but too many of us feared.
Our guns sent them away,
but they'll be back another day . . .

I think they would have stayed,
but too many people prayed,
too many cast a stone,
we're too protective of our home.

If they're going to come to us,
surely we should show some trust.
They're the brains out there after all,
they didn't have to come at all.

If they're going to travel space,
surely killing us is a waste?
They'll see that we are brave
when we put our guns aside and wave.

Richard Fox

A TRACERY OF TREES

Patterned against a liquid sky,
Black lace with gold-edge boughs entwined.
A tracery of trees . . . sharp etched,
By February's pen designed.

Dipped in the light of sinking sun,
Bare branches reaching to the glow
They stood in calm expectancy
Of morrow's hail, or rain, or snow.

In passing I their beauty saw
And yet cannot find words to write
What feelings flared up in my soul,
Uplifted by their splendid sight.

E Balmain

THE WATERFALL

Standing beneath the waterfall
Sunlit droplets, as they fall
Water trickling down my spine
Feelings that are quite divine

Sitting here in clear blue
Thoughts, of making love with you
Fill my head with passions deep
Desires I would like to keep!

Summer sun is shining through
Prisms, with their colourful hue
Sensual touch for me to feel
Warming me, from head to heel

Clinging silk upon my skin
Shapely flesh shows within
Water flowing over me
Naked breasts for you to see

Water kissing on my lips
Gently caressing both my hips
Hands, that have a gentle touch
These feelings, that I love so much!

Imagine you are by my side
Sensual passions deep inside
Underwater we will dine
Hearts and souls, have now entwined

The waterfall is there for me
To give me thoughts, of being free
My passions there are not to hide
Sensual thoughts, from deep inside

Ester Francisca Caruana

BLUEBELL WOOD

You do not need to tell me -
    I know that dance
    And could not though I tried.

Flesh boned to the other ground.
Quite right - never had the grace,
A beat too self-aware.

I'm telling myself I'm here

On an errand to pick bluebells
When I'm looking for the sisters
Sent to find faggots ages back
In Bluebell Wood.

One came back a changeling.

(What are these green antennae in my hair?)

Fettered about the feet.
    - O yes. I know that dance
    Turning strained skin to silver -

It's as well now. And all's well.
The hobbled changeling goes

A different step.

There was no way of knowing in the wood.

Moyra Stewart Wyllie

THE ROAD HOME

A lithesome pillar against overcast skies,
I saw you on the moor,
Sweep sinuous hills with stormcloud eyes
For the way home.
Heaven's glory you did not seek
Upon those desolate moors,
But in that quiet grave how shallow the sleep
To be at peace, yet not find rest.
So long a shadow in a realm of silence
Numbed by time and earth,
Yet at the crossroads where the waters meet,
Moss and flowers in autumn glory
Hold court for you in a beauteous nook
Of rugged bank and rippling brook;
And amongst the purple-brown sweeps,
A candle flame burns bright,
In a window aglow with love's undying light
From those parted long ago;
There to welcome you at the end of your roam
On this final stretch of the road home.

Rebecca Osborne

POLINA

We sat in the Metabolic Ward
On a June evening,
Playing Scrabble
While the sun went down.
She wore a negligée
Trimmed with lace,
And laughed happily,
Looking forward to her wedding.

We sat near a window
In the evening sun,
Alone except for a woman
On the telephone,
Who talked for ever;
The other patients
Were in the television room;
Time stood still.

And I had the strange feeling
Of being there for a moment
And at the same time
Of being there eternally -
So that even after her death
We are still in the metabolic ward,
Playing Scrabble on a June evening,
Shortly before her wedding.

Dorothy Buyers

PLAYING THE VOWEL GAME CIRCA 1960

AEIOU they're chanting
The vowels they number five
Teacher in the classroom chalking on the board
Children in the Junior School write it in their books
AEIOU they have to get it right
It's essential to their grammar
See how good it looks
AEIOU they're chanting AEIOU
They are putting pen to paper in the Junior School
AEIOU is their Golden Rule
AEIOU they're shouting 12345
They are playing the Vowel Game
They memorise the letters on which their words are built
AEIOU it has a lovely lilt
They chant it in the classroom of the Junior School
The teacher wipes it off the board
But they have it in their books
Look how neat it looks
They have it in their books
AEIOU 12345
AEIOU they're shouting, it's their Golden Rule
AEIOU in the Junior School
They are playing the Vowel Game
AEIOU 12345
The vowels they number five
It's the Vowel Game.

G Hatton

MAGICAL MOON

Oh beautiful moon, shining bright,
Covering the earth with your ethereal light,
Encompassing everything you see,
Bathing all in tranquillity.

You cast down your radiant glow
On humans and animals here below.
All feel safe under your magical spell
Which you and the stars emit so well.

Your beams reach down and caress the lake,
Dancing rhythmically until the dawn break.
They touch the leaves of the slender trees
Which sway in time to the gentle breeze.

All is peaceful, all is still
As you shine from above at God's will.
Whilst I below in awesome wonder
Stand and survey you way up yonder.

Patricia M Tudor

SEEKERS

They've hidden in corners
Or behind a chair,
Even under the bed
Before the drawers were there.

Inside the wardrobe
And then on top,
Was fine until discovery
Made that a flop!

Each year it gets harder
To find a place,
For them to hide
In a temporary space.

They've tried bags and boxes
As a disguise -
But sadly been found
By the wily and wise.

Like hide and seek
This game 'evergreen',
Is especially about
Not being seen!

Strange how the 'seekers'
All year cannot find
Things they are asked for
Because it's a bind!

Only at Christmas
Do the 'seekers' apply,
All of their skills
To retrieve what's put by.

Bright-coloured parcels
Lying in wait -
For Santa to come
Before it's too late!

Susan Green

A FEW DAYS TOGETHER

We had a few days together, you and I.
The first born - Number One Sun!
Recalling events long consigned to memory
Dusted off and relived as though it were only yesterday.

How well I remember your first few hours.
Amongst the noise and cries of other infants
You slept! Tiny fingers clenched into tiny fist -
A silent protest against the world.

School years, school reports - 'Good potential,
Must work harder.' What did they know!
You lived in a world of your own making,
Expanding your mind beyond their boundaries!

And so you left behind the dreaming years
To graduate in the University of Life -
Marriage, Mortgage and Maybees - still, I suspect,
With fist clenched silently against life's uncertainties.

'Why Number One Sun?' I heard you ask.
'Because you bring warmth and light into my life.'
You smiled and held my hand. We walked in silence
I pleased to spend time with my daughter, and you . . . ?

Natalie Clarke

LOVE

It may be a tear
That stabs you straight in the heart
But I'd rather deal with the pain
Than be torn apart
And
Have to pick up the pieces of a broken heart
As my love is true
Although often I may feel blue
But for love anything I would do.

Michelle Barnes

WAITING

Music that fills the long and weary hours,
Sheds shimmering light, to brighten darkened hearts,
While singing voices gently soothe,
And court a happier worthy muse.
So every sorrow quietly then departs,
To leave the gentle, fragrant scent of flowers.

Walking through flowers, magical as dreams,
The hours are flown as birds upon the wing,
Then eyes no longer shed their tears,
But clearly see the end of absence's fears,
And everywhere, the many voices sing,
A glorious burst of melody supreme.

This waiting, seeming without end,
Becomes an unreal territory apart,
Wherein to drift as gentle snow
Soundless upon earth below:
Like dreams that linger in the heart,
Bloom, as the flowers with the summer blend.

This drifting dream goes slowly by,
In shades of grey, but sometimes glows,
With rays of hope, that send a light,
Sparked off by music's soft delight,
For passing shadows only show,
The waiting soon will die.

Mary Hughes

BLIND DATE

In anticipation of love,
The hair is done,
The face made up,
The lady is nervous,
For the blind date is on.
Romantic thoughts,
Enter the man's mind,
As he wears a carnation,
Only recognizable to her.
The meal is booked,
Champagne for two,
He eagerly awaits,
Her entrance is due.
The evening ends,
A friendly embrace,
A kiss on the cheek,
As love adorns,
Her smiling face.
She hopes the blind date,
Has led to love,
But the man has decided,
That love can wait.

Martin Westcott

AUTUMN

Autumn, the bell that tolls for summer,
Heralds winter's stranglehold on life.
Yet goes, not with faint heart, but celebration,
As a bride entering the duties of a wife!

Autumn, when the blooms of summer's richness,
Fade, to lie beneath the chilling soil.
When, creatures of the wild, hide, sleeping,
Till springtime calls them, once again to toil.

Autumn, with a show of utmost splendour,
Colours our world, with leaves of every hue,
Crisping fallen ones, that carpet the path,
In the frost of the early morning dew!

Autumn, when the wind blows with a vengeance,
Fog and rain compete for status quo,
While sunsets, are glorious to gaze on,
And starry nights, set your heart aglow.

Autumn bids farewell, with technicoloured leaves,
That paint poetic pictures in your mind,
Making it the loveliest of seasons
Tho' it's about to leave the summer months behind!

Autumn then, strips those leaves,
Till trees, stand, stark and bare,
To embrace winter's snowy shroud,
And ghost-like frosty stare!

E M Eagle

UNEASY SPIRIT

I went to view a cottage, early one June morn;
A mist hung over all the lake, and swirled around the lawn.
Then suddenly a vision of a lady I did see,
And she was softly weeping, she quite enraptured me.
She was so young and beautiful, and in such deep despair,
I longed to ease her sorrow, and touch her long blonde hair.
So I followed at a distance, saw her fall on to her knees,
I heard her plaintive sobbing, come sighing on the breeze.
I hurried close up to her, but she had vanished where she fell,
And I found the crumbling ruins of an old and disused well.

The landlord of the local inn, solved the mystery for me,
It would seem the cottage owner, had a little girl aged three.
One day the infant vanished, and the lady in despair,
Drowned herself within the lake, the pain she could not bear.
We went back with equipment, to explore that well so deep,
And we found a tiny body, preserved as if in sleep.
We laid that baby down to rest, by her mother's side,
As grey clouds shed their silent tears, and wind around us sighed.
Then I left that quiet village, I didn't buy the lease,
But I hope the spirits of the lady, and her child, now rest in peace.

Kathleen Hill

WHERE WOULD I BE WITHOUT ME KIDS

I've wiped their bums and snotty noses
Played peek-a-boo and tickled toes
Looked for monsters under beds
Put lotions and potions on infested heads
I've made costumes for fairies, cats and dogs
Princesses destined to be kissed by frogs
Witches, mummies, ghosts and ghouls
All complete with whatever tools
I've baked cakes, made Easter bonnets
Done English homework - written sonnets
Helped with maths and geometry
Fetched umpteen balls from out the tree
I've paced the floor when they were unwell
Kept the secrets they couldn't tell
I've explained about the birds and bees
Their laughter brought me to my knees
I've polished shoes and ironed shirts
Upped and downed the hems on skirts
Made paper models and stuff with glue
Peeled spuds - an acre or two
I've striven to keep them safe from harm
Though they managed many a broken leg or arm
I've stayed awake when they were late
Worried like hell when they had a date
Wiped the tears when things went wrong
Kept up to date with the latest song
Lent to them my listening ear
Praised the day that they all left school
And hoped by then they'd learned the rule

And yet, I find my youth long gone
And still the chores they carry on
Whilst these my children live here no more
They still come tapping at my door
Can you lend or will you give
These are my children after said and done
All grown up and having fun
But oh I wish they would leave me be
To have some time now - *just for me*

Jan Penn

ENGLAND 2001

England 2001, spring had come,
On a cold rainy day,
Lambs were dying in fields of clay.
Farmers unable to help because of foot and mouth.
Gunshots over hills and valleys,
Lorries roar past with covered sides,
Hide their cargo from human eyes.
Signs say pathways closed
The countryside is out of bounds.

Smoke drifts through the trees,
In a field where daffodils once grew,
A deep trench long and wide,
Is filling up with dead inside.
Bulldozers are busy filling in,
Men in white are disinfecting everything.
Travelling down the country lanes,
Signs say pathways closed,
The countryside is out of bounds.

Sandra Wood

SUNDAY AFTERNOON TELEVISION

The Britten Quartet takes to the air
Black leather jackets
Beside The Thames
The viola player ties back his hair.

The Britten Quartet takes to the air
In deep plain shirts
Schubert is popular
Each in a modern wiggle-back chair.

The Britten Quartet takes to the air
Plate glass windows
Beethoven middle and late
Designer shirts are worn with flair.

The Britten Quartet takes to the air
Columns in space
Exquisite Ravel
This quartet could never be square.

Marjorie Lloyd

RISING TIDES

How often does the current take you under,
or the sea whisper,
whisper your name?
How often did you dip a toe,
and never feel the same,
how often do the tides change,
to match a passing feeling,
or sea air fill your heart and soul,
invoking a new meaning?
How often do white horses call,
pollution from your head,
how quickly do I regret,
everything I said?
How often does the ocean wash,
a host of tears away?
The ocean's healing spirit,
draws me here to stay.
I cross my legs and dig my toes,
into golden sandy beach,
how come I find the answers now,
when they were out of reach?
Rising tides, back and forth,
raging breath of earth,
give to me my answers,
give to me second birth.

A Denby

HERE COMES SUMMER

Summer is here so let's raise a cheer
Gone is winter and days so drear.
Warm sunny days to laze in the sun
And relax in the evening when work is done.

Some of us head for the sea and the coast
And do the things we like to do most
Many travel abroad and journey far
Others like to stay nearer and travel by car.

Whatever our choice we all need a break
As to our destination our way we make.
Just to take it easy is what we plan to do
And forget work for the time being - so it's up to me and you.

Marjorie Ridley

TRUE IDENTITY

Dominant brown buds
Perfectly formed
Their embryo awaiting birth,
Scales slowly unfurl revealing magnolia florets
Unspoilt
like a new babe.
Born
into a polluted world, guarded by soft foliage
this arboreal queen dominates.
Clad in
glorious majesty
any imperfections are masked. Age worn
conifers debased by chestnuts' youthful verdure,
as she reaches out to
praise her maker.
True identity is not revealed
in splendid raiment but in
power
to withstand the storm.

Wendy Dedicott

CAN I STAY?

Granny can I stay with you,
Can I stay the week,
I love the way you play with me,
Especially hide and seek.
Mummy is always busy,
And she has no time right now,
Can you ask her if I can stay,
I'll be good I'll show you how.
I'll help you with the washing up,
I'll help you with the dusting,
So Granny can I stay with you
For Mummy wouldn't mind,
I'm sure she really will say yes
And leaving me behind.

Jean Lloyd-Williams

HOPE IS ALL AROUND

Open your eyes, look and see,
Under the horizon,
And above the sea,
The first rays of hope cast upon the water,
Birds spread their wings through the air,
Butterflies glide like controlled kites,
Nature is around quietly, secretly but ever present,
Hope is present in nature, within nature we have hope,
Images of hope surround us every day,
The planets rotate the sun,
Humans breathe,
Children are born,
Different species of animals are present,
Open your eyes, look and see,
We see life therefore we can keep hope alive.

Sana Arshad

AFTER THE 'OP'

Pick up those crutches
And get down the road
Call in at Tescos
And bring back a load
Some food for you
And food for me
Food for breakfast
Lunch, dinner and tea
Roast chicken for lunch
And maybe some rice
Perhaps ice cream for afters
That would be nice
But if it is raining
Mind you don't slip
Or you will be back in hospital
Waiting for a second new hip

Diana Daley

HOLIDAY IN BLACKPOOL

We've just had a holiday in Blackpool
Blackpool, the famous holiday resort
Favourite of the North and others
Entertainment for all the family
Sandy beaches, roller coasters and rides
Famed for its entertainment
With shows of comedy, dancing, music
And many other tourist attractions
Its mighty tower, a famous landmark
Its Victorian ballroom, still with its
Mighty, moving wurlitzer organ
Its three long piers and shows
The Tower circus and attractions
Consistently drawing thousands
Then of course, the countless lights
Dazzling, a blaze of colours
Stretching the length of the promenade
Blinking on and off, as if to move

Terry Daley

THE GREATEST!

What poet immortal, could measure his rhyme?
Most certainly, no one, in this modern time!
His wisdom, so certain, so sure and so true,
In words unsurpassable, but to a few!
And they, in their failure - to read to the end,
Tis no wonder, they could not, for sure - comprehend!

Honour'd by country, but not half enough!
This bard was the best, though his manner was rough!
Often blamed by his critics, his life was a sin;
Yet that life was quite natural - as for his kin!
Common and poor and yet still richly pleasant;
In poetry, the words, of this truly great peasant!

His name shall go on, to the halls of great fame;
Though his life, to so many, was so full of shame!
'Our Rabbie' remembered, through year after year,
In the land of the heather, the hills and the deer!
In that Sassenach Land, he may oft be forgot,
And treated as one of the commoner's lot!

Still the greatest of all, as one century turns,
There never was better - than 'Our Rabbie Burns!'

R Bissett

ONE WAY OR ANOTHER

The wounds of battle, of husband and wife,
May only last days, but thoughts are for life.
The words you use, sting each other's mind,
They're often not true, but hurtful you'll find.
Your nose may be bleeding, lips all sore,
The heart is destroyed, the mind red raw.
Pains of your passion, only you'll ever know,
They won't leave, and won't let you go.
But somehow between you, find compromise,
Or else to your boxes, you'll only despise.
When all is calm, both figure it out,
Either part then that day, or turn it about.
Before this day, throughout the calms,
Forget not the bad, nor also their charms.
We are the healers, of our own heartaches,
Time is a concept, and how long it takes.

Geoffrey Woodhead

IN THE SHRINE CHURCH

Leaning against this pillar,
I watch pale sunlight
Flicker and fade
On gaudy gilt of candlesticks,
Gold crucifix,
And plaster saints,
Strangely sad in their tinselled finery.
A few pilgrims
Stray through the long nave,
Lost sheep, bewildered by so much glory.
Some kneel,
Some stand,
Looking up awkwardly,
Embarrassed,
Ill at ease
With their fierce God;
While the tall nun
With the frozen smile
Bustles about, arranging this and that,
And a small child wails,
Imprisoned in its reins.

Jackie Lapidge

THE BEAUTY OF THE CLOUDS

When you sit and look at the clouds,
the beauty that forms in the sky.
You see the sun shining bright,
and the beautiful birds just passing by.

As those clouds go sailing by,
Pictures seem to form in your mind,
That one over there looks like a dinosaur,
Words for this beauty we cannot find.

The one over there looks like a face,
Is it the face of God or one of my friends.
Even if we cannot think of who to us it reminds,
We know all this beauty to us God sends.

Sometimes these clouds look so dark and grey,
And it brings down those showers of rain.
Thunder, lightning, all this takes place
Yet in our minds beautiful thoughts remain.

But without the beauty of those clouds,
There would be nothing to see as we look up above,
So remember the beauty as you look at the clouds
Saying thank you to God for his gifts and love.

Carole Osselton

CONJECTURES

Scientists suggest that Earth is lucky to be here
Planet Earth days are numbered they fear

Other planets have taken the brunt of giant meteors so far
Planet Earth seems to have a mysterious guiding star

Scientists also suggest that the sun may get too close
Then planet Earth will eventually roast

Big black holes may cause the sun's demise
The sun disappearing in one such hole clockwise

Earth's existence is linked to the sun for sure
Hopefully big black holes will continue to give the sun a detour

These conjectures may not happen in a million years
So put on hold any serious fears

Humans may be first to instigate Earth's destruction
World leaders hold the key to Earth's continuation.

Brian Bates

INTERNATIONAL

The enemies of a nation
Are not the sister and brother
Who breathe
God's breath of living
In a foreign place,
But unforgiving ideologies
Devised by men
Promoting domination
Of one race over another,
And holding hands in many lands
They threaten God's creation.
Concealed in nationalism
The lust for power
Is revealed in the crimes
Of history,
Where through the years
Its pursuit has brushed
Cities and men to dust
Without shedding even ash tears,
Nationalism with its blood stained sword
Has no seat
At the table of the Lord,
For the Kingdom of the Almighty
Is and always shall be
International.

Pat Isiorho

WILD THING!

Smoke rises from dry land, high into the sky.
As my eyes fill with a picture of an African Tapestry.
Sun rise peeking over the horizon, a
movement of grey walking forward.

The sound of thunder rolling under
ground, speaking to the spirits, forty miles to
Kariba.
After the rain is spent, crickets chirp and birds
sing their song.

Passing the smoke that thunders, through the
wildness of drums beating.
On past the Zimbabwean ruins, a journey close
to the wild.

Rolling in pools of mud, their faith never
quivering under the heat.
Keeping a watchful eye out for the predators spying
their daily movements in the long dry grass.

A picture to behold forever and beyond.

Bridget Drinkwater

TOUCHING MEMORIES

Observe my present, learn about my past,
Like a child you drink it in
Yearning for more information,
Searching for more clues,
You want to be near, understand
Who made me so unforgiving,
So suspicious and so mistrusting.
But look closely, they're absent
A forgotten nightmare.
Too traumatic to remember.
They are only for me, my demons
Shut away to protect you
Like a soft cotton wool blanket
Enveloping your heart
Keeping it warm and true,
Not a victim of calculation and venom
From those who would hurt you.
My pictures introduce my friends not foes,
Genuine people of trust and loyalty
Look in their faces, smile with recognition
That reality has not misguided their understanding
Of what is right and wrong, good or evil.
Reach out, touch them, they won't bite,
Just images of happier times.
Ask me about the story each photo tells
And you might discover me,
I may let you in, but not to help
The pain is mine alone.
I need to solve the puzzle,
You want to be the missing piece
But that space was filled and then lost
It will now remain forever empty.

You are my complete picture and
Soon the memory of you will take its place
Amongst those who taught me
How to love again.

Jennifer Matthews

HOLIDAY IN MENTON

Nice skies over Menton
Blue Mediterranean seas
Jean Cocteau's spirit
Lies easy in his castle
There's the slightest breeze.

Boats are in the harbour
At the quay Napoleon III
Everywhere tall palm trees
Embrace Technicolor skies.

The beach is choked with people
Their bodies burn all day
A few of them mahogany
The rest as red as clay.

Early in the morning
The tramps are sleeping rough
One by Espace 2000
His trolley full of stuff.

The orange trees are beautiful
Who could ever have enough
Of blue skies and bright sunshine
And all that kind of guff?

Rupert Smith

SUMMERSAULT OF RUGBY

A cup of coffee,
a piece of cake.
The café is bubbling
with sounds people make.

The chomp of teeth,
the clatter of plates.
Everyone is talking,
complaining about fate.

No need to look around.
The food smells devine.
I taste the house fusilli.
I'll be back another time!

Saturday shoppers
with arms so laden
retreat to Summersault's,
the town's food haven.

They come on in
and settle down.
The first taste of coffee,
the worries have flown.

A moment to relax
and take a look around
at the gift-lined walls.
The clocks make no sound.

I enjoyed my coffee
while reading *Poetry Now,*
But I shall have to go,
I have a lawn to mow.

Angela G Pearson

RESPONSIBILITY

Can we own a land?
Can we own a bit of England?
Can we leave a place better than we found it?
Our artificial identity that we place on places.
Put aside our acres, and our differences,
Our own security in the land we think we have.
Affirming what we think we are.
Then let's face responsibility to what
We should become,
And aim for a better world,
A united goal,
Everyone working together,
While around us
Are increasing signs of insecurity
In this age of social change.

Paul Darby

SNOW MAN

You're looking out of the window,
you're watching the settling snow.
Soft the snow falls like angels' feathers,
bringing your children and joy together.

For they're building a snowman,
from whatever snow that they can.
They give me a nose, eyes, hat and pipe,
so tell me now, what do I look like?

You say I am always still and cold,
stood here for all of you to behold,
but that was the way that I was made.
This is what I am, happy in the shade.

Then there was a break in the clouds,
and the great sun shines out loud,
hurting me, until I do cry,
until I melt, wither and die.

The sun is here and I've nowhere to go,
my tears run cold, turned from snow,
Until all that is left is my eyes of coal,
and my hat dancing in the wind, with my soul.

Dale Mullock

SUBMISSIONS INVITED
SOMETHING FOR EVERYONE

POETRY NOW 2002 - Any subject,
any style, any time.

WOMENSWORDS 2002 - Strictly women,
have your say the female way!

STRONGWORDS 2002 - Warning!
Age restriction, must be between 16-24,
opinionated and have strong views.
(Not for the faint-hearted)

All poems no longer than 30 lines.
Always welcome! No fee!
Cash Prizes to be won!

Mark your envelope (eg *Poetry Now) 2002*
Send to:
Forward Press Ltd
Remus House, Coltsfoot Drive,
Peterborough, PE2 9JX

**OVER £10,000 POETRY PRIZES
TO BE WON!**

Judging will take place in October 2002